3 Key Strategies to Financial Success

Practical and Biblical Principles to Financial Success

THOMAS JONES &

TERRI B. JONES

ISBN-13: 978-1517743956
ISBN-10: 1517743958

WORKBOOK DEDICATION

This workbook is dedicated to my mother Delores White (deceased). I saw my mother work two and three jobs to ensure that our family (four boys and one girl) had the natural things needed in life such as a roof over our head, a bed to sleep in with clean linen, clean clothes and food to eat. She also made sure that we had a spiritual foundation in the midst of her busy life. I am the spirit filled and financially savvy woman today because of the legacy of my mother. I hope this publication inspire the third and fourth generation of our family line. Also, I give thanks to my husband because of his continued support of everything that God has blessed me to do. Lastly, I thank God, my Lord and Saviour Jesus Christ for the Holy Spirit that leads and guides me in all things that I set out to do and pursue.

OVERVIEW

Who is this for? This workbook can be used by individuals, couples or groups. It is designed to give practical and biblical principles to their financial success and wealth building.

Each chapter of this workbook has the following components:

- A topic
- A scripture
- A prayer
- A case study or example
- An assignment
- A worksheet to complete

Online modules with audio, transcript pdf and downloads can be found on the membership website http://tjandtjenterprise.com/join

Join our online private Facebook Group at
http://facebook.com/afamilyhelpingfamilies

If you would like to book the "90/10 Steward – I Love Therefore I Give" live workshop, details are located at http://iloveigive.com/registration

CONTENTS

ACKNOWLEDGMENTS

I give honor to every single person seeking a mate as well as newly married couples for your willingness to be good stewards over the number one cause of divorces – **money**. Your investment in this workbook shows that you are a person of action and not just words. You not only "say" you love but you are willing to demonstrate that same love to God, yourself and others and leave a legacy of **true love** in the world.

I LOVE THEREFORE I GIVE INTRODUCTION

Hello and welcome to The Three Key Strategies to Financial Success Workbook. These key strategies will be taught using **"The 90/10 Steward – I Love Therefore I Give"** financial success training. Are you a success oriented, self-motivated and positive thinking individual. Do you truly have the desire to create an awesome life for yourself, the kingdom of

God and others? If this describes you, then you are at the right place at the right time connected to the right people. As you indulge yourself into this training, you will have the light within you turned on to discover your financial wealth that is tied to your purpose here on earth.

In this training and within the online membership site is a culmination of the actual experiences and revelation on finances given to us by the Holy Spirit to educate, empower and enlighten you to become an end times financier in the kingdom of God. **End times financiers** are *those God will use as a conduit, a portal, a channel, a modern day Joseph and distribution center to release his blessings upon to fulfill His purpose.* Therefore, you will be positioned to reap the **end times harvest of souls** through the divine strategic **favor of God** in the midst of an open window, open heaven and open door.

As end times financiers, our assignment is to make you aware of the 3 key strategies to empower you to **lovingly give to God, yourself and others** as you lose the chains of debt, bring an end to financial bondage and redirect those same resources to obtain generational wealth.

As you move by faith, walk in obedience and trust God, you will position yourself to experience the financial breakthrough needed to:

- Move from blindness to 20/20 vision to see your way out of financial ruin
- Super impose God's will over the kingdom of this world
- Break the generational curse of poverty in your life and anybody who comes in contact with you
- Stop giving the flesh all the pleasures that deprive you of supernatural blessings
- Repair the waste places in your community, your state and this great nation
- Quit being afraid of going to the mailbox, answering your phone or door
- Build generational wealth to pass down to the 3rd and 4th generation
- Resurrect your family money anointing
- Set financial goals and finally accomplish them
- Breathe life into your financial decisions
- Have a solid retirement plan
- Have enough liquid money available when needed
- Access your blessings through faith, prayer and the simple act of obedience with everything you do
- Finally unlock the gift within you to do the thing that you are already purposed, predestined and love to do
- Proclaim the good news that the financial enemy you see today, you will see no more forever!
- And More ...

Your investment in this training, let's us know you are ready to seize the moment and implement God's end time strategies and because of your zeal, my husband and I are serious about helping you in the process. Therefore, you will find everything we do in this workbook so you can duplicate our success.

You will find the online training consist of 4 simple to follow foundational modules. The online training (pdf's and mp3 audios) gives you the exact information, concepts and tasks you need to complete each success action step.

Then, if you need personal one-on-one guidance or help, we are available by phone or email. Just send an email to tjandtjenterprise@gmail.com. We want to eliminate every roadblock we know you will face and give you multiple ways to quickly and easily overcome those roadblocks.

As mentioned, this training is for individuals as well as groups. Please feel free to contact us to schedule a live workshop for your group or ministry. The live workshop is hands on, memorable, impacting and life changing. We work with all attendees one-on-one so they can walk away with a budget setup for the quarter, their debt elimination and wealth building plan of action to ensure their financial success as well as the tools to make this a part of their daily lifestyle.

The Key Ingredient Is YOU!

The 90/10 Steward – I Love Therefore I Give training has been proven to work for us and others in the body of Christ. That means **you** bring the key ingredient to the recipe for success.

Just to Be CLEAR...
The 90/10 Steward - I Love Therefore I Give training is not just another financial training. This training is about what **God wants to do NOW**, for now is the time for the sons of God to manifest and establish God's kingdom here on earth. It is time for a takeover and transfer of wealth to take place. Do not delay in obedience.

We have been positioned to take back the wealth our parents should have had, our grandparents should have had and what is rightfully ours by God's design. The body of Christ has been graced by Almighty God to receive this wealth but **the foundation must be laid first**. This is where the 90/10 Steward - I Love Therefore I Give training comes into perspective.

This training is foundational in the sense that it teaches you through the

Word of God biblical and practical principles to lay the foundation to prepare you to handle the wealth, know what to do with the wealth and stay humbly in the will of God despite the wealth. It is a resource that includes step by step instructional worksheets to accompany success action steps.

As one 90/10 Steward client, Malvin Jones puts it, *"I was just thinking that this was going to be another one of those get rich quick seminars but to my surprise, it was nothing close to being what I thought. The thing I liked most about this training was that everything they taught, they were able to back it up with the Word of God. This is what set this workshop apart."*

Another 90/10 Steward client, Eloyce Forrest says *"The workshop was so much fun and very informational for financial success God's Way! Your prayer at the beginning of the class was a divine transfer of what you and your husband has experienced firsthand of God's great wealth transfer. It was a pleasure to be a part and thank you for inviting me to "change" and the opportunity to experience financial peace and health. I look forward to the next class and will do my best to invite others. As we all continue on the path to God's plan to prosper and be in good health, I pray that each and every endeavor the Lord has for you and your family be magnified to the next level. We are the generation of the great wealth transfer and I declare we shall be "Holy Millionaires!" I prophesy!"*

There are other testimonies but I don't want to focus on them, I want to help you have a testimony. So, will you be committed to following through to the end of the training? Or are you going to let "life" get in the way and keep you from doing and achieving what you were already purposed and pre-destined to do before the foundations of the world?

Throughout this training, we include specific exercises to help you position yourself to accomplish your goals. All you need to do is take advantage of them and put them into action as you go through the training.

What to Expect...
If you are new to budgeting, saving and investing, but willing to put in 1 to 2 hours of easy consistent focused actions monthly, it is realistic to have your foundational pieces in place to start seeing successful results in your first 90 days. Then you will see even greater results in 6 months and by the end of a 12 month period, you will definitely have a testimony of reaching and surpassing financial goals.

If you are already having financial success, then you can couple it with our expertise and grow your existing portfolio exponentially. By following a proven step-by-step system, you can get started and moving with momentum significantly faster and easier than you have in the past. You will know exactly what to do, the order to do it in and why to do it.

I look forward to hearing about your financial success! Let's get started.

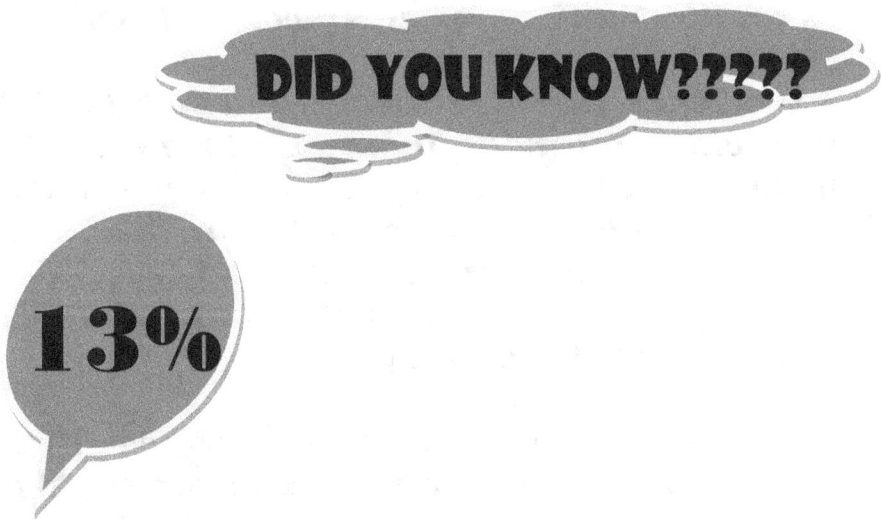

According to an LA Times publication, more than **two-thirds of married men** say they make investment decisions, for the most part on their own. However, **only 13 percent** of married women agree their partner is the main decision maker.

43%

In a survey of couples, around 4 out of 10 (**43 percent**) say they make investment decisions for retirement together.

"A budget tells us what we can't afford, but it doesn't keep us from buying it."
William Feather

MOST PEOPLE BUDGETING PROCESS:

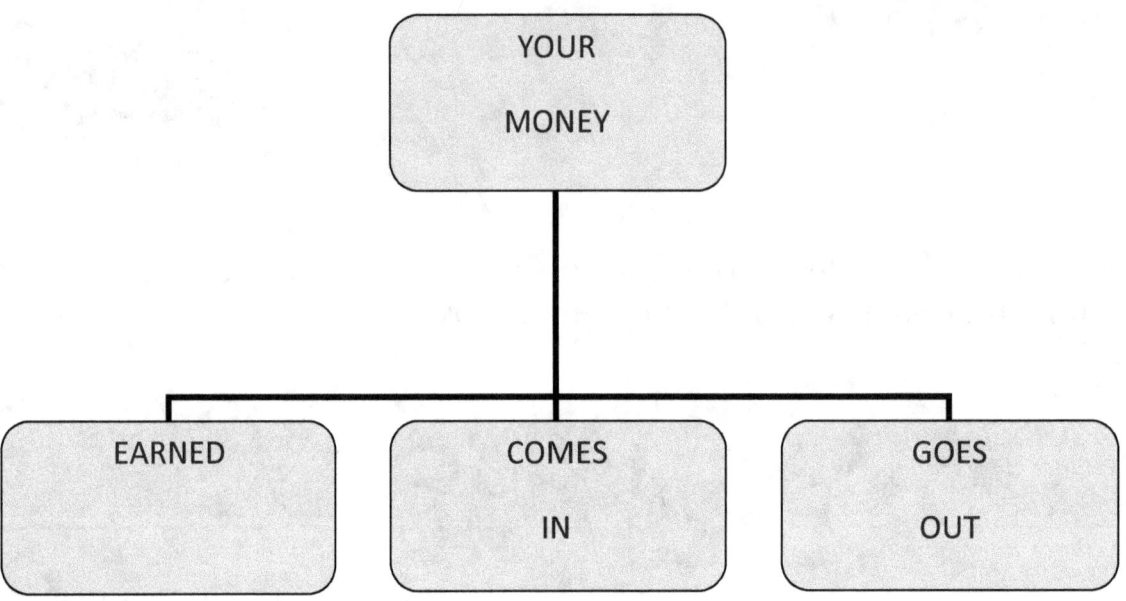

Let's work on getting a new perspective on money and budgeting to achieve financial success!

In this training on family budgeting, saving and wealth building, we will answer the key question:

☐ Why have a family budget?

☐ Why do you need a family budget?

☐ What is the rationale behind family budgeting?

☐ What are the benefits and advantages of a family budget?

We will elaborate more on each question throughout this workbook. For the most part, people believe that a family budget is the equivalent of this process: **money is earned and comes in; money is spent and moves out!**

Families have diverse reasons and motivations for budgeting. Briefly summarized, here are some reasons people budget:

☐ To gain control of their financial life, monthly bills and spending

☐ Be prepared and avoid surprises

☐ Save for a major purchase

☐ Opt out of a vicious circle of ever-spiraling debt or spend-now-pay-later thinking

☐ Expand their lifestyle(s)

☐ Retire early

☐ Eliminate money as a source of tension and topic for argument

☐ Becoming self-reliant and empowered to know that debt does not rule their lives anymore!

Now is the time for implementation not procrastination. Ready? Let's start with the three foundational key strategies for financial success.

Retirement Plan A	**Retirement Plan B**

1 THE THREE FOUNDATIONAL KEY STRATEGIES

In this training, I'm going to be sharing with you kingdom financial principles from the word of God so grab your Bible, a pen and paper.

MISSION: Enlighten you through the word of God to implement the 3 **powerful key strategies** to execute discipline in your finances to become debt free and redirect those same resources to build generational wealth to become a 90/10 steward and end time financier.

SCRIPTURE: John 3:16 *"For God so loved the world that he gave his only begotten son that whosoever believeth in him should not perish but have everlasting life." KJV*

TOPIC: The Three Foundational Key Strategies

PRAYER: Dear Heavenly Father, thank you for this day, thank you for being our Lord and Savior. Thank you for the wisdom, knowledge and understanding you have given us in the area of finances. Help us to be good stewards over everything you have placed in our possession. Help us to bring glory to your name as we establish your kingdom on earth as it is in

Blank Sheet of Paper

heaven. Let us walk out our destiny and purpose as we take dominion, subdue, multiply, replenish and be fruitful in all that we set out to do. In Jesus Name Amen.

EVALUATION: Now what I want you to do right now is print out **the sheet of paper (page 20) included in this training** and get a pen. Then I want you to draw a line down the middle of that sheet of paper. Now on the left side of the line I want you to write down what your life was like before you accepted Jesus Christ as your Lord and Saviour.

Now if you were a liar write it down, angry, stingy, alcoholic, impulsive, hooked prescription drugs, walked in fear, lazy, depressed all the time, used to curse like a sailor, ungrateful.

Now on the right hand side of the line I want you to write down what your life is like now that Jesus has come into your heart – if you are lovable now, dependable, exercise self- control, thankful, compassionate, forgiving, full of joy, faithful, walking in obedience, truthful, make wise decisions, using your God given creativity to generate wealth.

Now let's take a moment to thank God for salvation and transforming us into his image and all of the benefits and blessing that are at our disposal. Amen. Hallelujah, thank you Jesus, thank you Lord.

Now the reason I had you to reflect on what your life was like before Christ and what your life is like now is so that you can see that you already have the power to be a 90/10 steward for Philippians 4:13 says *"I can do all things through Christ which strengthens me."* Now let me give you the background of the 90/10 steward.

BACKGROUND: My husband and I were speakers at a Kingdom

Millionaire Summit in Greenville, Alabama. We were invited to speak on becoming a kingdom millionaire. During my time of preparation, God instructed me to make it clear to the attendees that if they weren't good stewards over the $4,000 a month they were receiving already, God was not going to entrust them with millions. And now that we are in a recession or shall I say our economic system is not at its best, do you know that there are individuals that are maintaining billionaire status as we speak?

Now I don't know if you ever watch CNBC News but every year, they announce the names of some of the wealthiest people of the last quarter for each year. Bill Gates and Warren Buffet are normally somewhere in the top 3 positions but the one that I want to point out is a young man by the name of Mark Zuckerberg because at the age of 26, he was in position 35 because his income of $6 billion dollars had increased by 245% from the previous year. Just in case you don't know who Mark Zuckerberg is, I will tell you who he is – he is the person who started the social media platform Facebook.

Facebook has several million free users utilizing this social platform. Now you might be wondering, how he generated over $6B from a product that is free to utilize. Well, I don't know if this young man is saved or not but he tapped into his creativity and offers free signup to Facebook to all of its users but charges the advertisers for the ads on Facebook.

I said all of that to say, if this young man can accomplish such a massive goal, we as children of the most high God, can do similar things and even more through Jesus Christ as end time financiers.

As defined earlier, an end time financier is one who God is preparing to set apart before Christ returns to pour out His wealth and blessing upon to use as a conduit to finance the kingdom in order to reap the end time harvest of souls.

90/10 STEWARD: Now, let me introduce you to the 90/10 steward. A 90/10 steward is a Christian who loves the Lord, has spiritual wisdom as well as practical financial wisdom. This love is evident by reciprocating the

 same love given to us back to God, yourself and others. The spiritual wisdom is evident by a Christian operating in obedience to the Word of God with their finances. The practical financial wisdom is evident by the Christian implementing discipline with their finances.

The 90/10 Steward – I Love Therefore I Give teaching has 3 key foundational strategies. **The first key foundational strategy** is based on the love demonstrated in John 3:16. Let's look at John 3:16 which says ***"For God so loved the world that he gave his only begotten son that whosoever believeth in him should not perish but have everlasting life."*** As God demonstrated his love by giving of his most prized treasure, our Lord and Saviour Jesus Christ, we are to reciprocate that same selfless giving of love. We have been created in His image, His likeness and similitude, so we have within us the ability to demonstrate that same love.

The second foundational key strategy for the 90/10 steward is to love God enough to obediently give tithes of 10% based on Malachi 3:10. Now let's look at Malachi 3:10 which says ***"Bring you all the tithes into the storehouse that there may be meat in my house and prove me now herewith saith the Lord of host if I will not open you the windows of heaven and pour you out a blessing that there shall not be room enough to receive it."***

So not only will we be blessed but everybody else we come in contact with will be blessed because of the overflow. And not only is He going to bless us but Malachi 3:11 says ***"And I will rebuke the devourer for your sakes and he shall not destroy the fruits of your ground neither shall your vine cast her fruit before the time in the field saith the Lord of host."*** This shows that not only is he going to bless us but He will keep the enemy from our blessing and lastly, Malachi 3:12 says ***"And all nations shall call you blessed for ye shall be a delightsome land saith the Lord of host."***

Now how many of us can say that when we visit our friends and families, when we go to our jobs, when we do business throughout our community that we are perceived as a blessing? Hopefully when people see you coming, they don't try to go another way to avoid you asking them for another $5.00 when you haven't paid them back the last $5 you borrowed from them.

Or are they glad to see you because they know you are going to pick up the tab for lunch or dinner or you'll bless them with the money to get their hair permed or you are going to slip a $20.00 bill into their pocket or purse. Yes we are blessed to be a blessing. When you walk in obedience and give the tithes and offerings to your local church and other Christian ministries, you are positioning yourself for a supernatural harvest.

 **The third foundational key strategy** for the 90/10 steward is being a wise and faithful steward with the 90% based on Luke 12:42. Let's look at Luke 12:42 which says *"And the Lord said, who then is that faithful and wise steward, whom his Lord shall make ruler over his household, to give them their portion of meat in due season?"*

Are you one that will implement the wisdom given by God to be faithful over everything you have been entrusted to oversee and to establish God's kingdom here on earth? We all have an assignment here on earth to fulfill. In order to fulfill this assignment, you are going to have to utilize one or all three of these to get your assignment done – your time, talent and/or treasure.

So, let me ask you these questions, have you been a good steward over your time? Do you know what you are talented to do? Are you implementing spiritual and practical financial wisdom with the treasures you have been blessed to steward? Our Lord & Saviour has put a lot of trust in us so we should not want to betray that trust.

So not only is it important for us to tithe but it is equally as important for us to use discipline with the 90% because the whole **100% belongs to God**. This means that the 90/10 steward is tithing **10%** of their income in obedience to **Malachi 3:10** and they are also a good steward over the **90%** based on **Luke 12:42**. All of this is driven by the love that we have for

God, ourselves and others.

So if you generate any type of income, whether it's from a 9-5 job, self-employment, unemployment, disability, social security or retirement you have seed to sow. For Genesis 8:22 says *"While the earth remaineth, seed time and harvest, cold and heat and summer and winter and day and night shall not cease."* There is no way on this earth you can reap a harvest without sowing. Sowing and reaping goes hand in hand. Even if "you" didn't sow, somebody else did.

And since you truly love the Lord, we aren't going to put a lot of discussion into tithing because experience has proven that where your heart is, that is where your treasure is. God demonstrated his love for us by giving his most treasured possession for the remission of our sins and Jesus obediently endured the cross. His nature is to give and he gives to us generously. His giving is perpetual.

Since we are created in his image we have the same power to demonstrate our love by giving from our heart our most treasured possession. Our giving should not be done out of obligation or a sense of duty but from a heart that is overflowing with love for our Heavenly Father. For Matthew 22:37-39 says *"Jesus said unto him, thou shalt love the Lord thy God with all thy heart and with all thy soul and with all your mind. This is the first and great commandment and the second is like unto it thou shalt love thy neighbor as thyself."*

STEWARD: Now let's look at the definition of a steward according to the Random House dictionary. A steward is **a person who manages another's property or financial affairs who administers anything as an agent for others.**

Now let's think about this, the Almighty God, the one who sits high and looks low, the one who owns the cattle on a thousand hills, all the gold is His, all the silver is His and everything that was made is His, He is the one who turns the hearts of kings, He sits one down and puts another one up. This God has entrusted us to be stewards of His wealth. Knowing this wouldn't you want to properly steward these possessions with financial wisdom?

Let's look at Psalms 8:3-8 which says in the NIV, *"When I consider your heavens, the work of your fingers, the moon and the stars which you have set in place what is man that you are mindful of him, the son of man that you care for him. You made him a little lower than the heavenly beings and crowned him with glory and honor. You made him ruler over the works of your hands, you put everything under his feet all flock and herbs and the beasts of the field, the birds of the air and the fish of the sea all that swim the paths of the seas."*

What an awesome honor and privilege to be a 90/10 steward. So let's decide today that we are going to be a wise and faithful steward as we implement wisdom and discipline over the things we have been entrusted to steward until our Lord and Saviour returns.

Now that we understand our role as a 90/10 steward and the three foundational keys, let's delve into our first assignment – **Part 1 - The Monthly Cashflow Statement.**

Blank Sheet of Paper

2 MONTHLY CASHFLOW STATEMENT

FIRST ASSIGNMENT: Now let's go over your first assignment - the Monthly Cashflow Statement.

PART 1 – THE MONTHLY CASHFLOW STATEMENT

You will use the Monthly Cashflow Statement each month as your budgeting system to track your finances along with the **Track It! Slips**.

Doing this assignment will help you create a budget based on the income you generate on a regular pay basis. Budgeting is a great practice if you are looking to prevent yourself from falling victim to overspending, insufficient funds and overdrafts. Also, creating a budget for yourself is a simple process and can help you to know what you have coming in and going out in order to keep you out of debt or even get you out of debt.

In order to create a budget, print the **Monthly Cashflow Statement** included in this training. Write down your pay week gross pay and net pay at the beginning of each pay period in the allotted fields. You will need to look at your pay statement to get this information. Because of technology, most places of employment provide pay statements online. So find out how to access your pay statements and print them each month for use with this assignment.

STUB SAMPLES INC.
4891 INGLESIDE DRIVE
HUNTINGTON BEACH CA 92649

Earnings Statement

EMPLOYEE NO.	EMPLOYEE NAME		SOCIAL SECURITY NO	PERIOD BEG.	PERIOD END	CHECK DATE
045345	JOHN J. DOE		xxx-xx-9898	01/16/2011	02/01/2011	02/04/2011

EARNINGS	HOURS	RATE	CURRENT AMOUNT	WITHOLDINGS/DEDUCTIONS	CURRENT AMOUNT	YEAR TO DATE
REGULAR PAY	87.60		2307.69	STATE TAX AMT	87.69	350.77
				DEFERRED CMP	0.00	0.00
				FED TAX AMT	281.54	1126.15
				HI TAX	33.46	133.85
				OASDI	96.92	387.69

CURRENT AMOUNT	CURRENT DEDUCTIONS	NET PAY	YTD EARNINGS	YTD DEDUCTIONS	YTD NET PAY	CHECK NO.
2307.69	499.62	1808.08	9230.77	1998.48	7232.31	48974

Pay Statement

Next you will write down 10% tithes, 5% offering, 5% fun, 10% savings and then 70% expenses in the appropriate fields. We will discuss the percentages of each expense in another chapter to determine what percentage of your take home pay is used for each expense.

Mortgage Expense Example: Take home pay (net pay) = **$1789**
Mortgage = **$800**
% of your net pay that should be allocated for rent/mortgage = **25-40%**
Actual % spent on mortgage is 45% (1789 x 45% = $805)

If the percentage allocated is outside of the range, do not fret; you can make adjustments with other expenses to allow for this difference.

NOTE: Please do not let this simple math deter you from budgeting. As you regularly populate your cashflow statement, the math will not be an issue.

10% of the 100% - Gross Pay VS Net Pay

Before we go any further, let me explain these percentages – once you determine your gross income by reviewing your pay statement, you are to tithe 10% of your **gross pay** instead of your **net pay**. The reason you want to tithe based on your gross income is because you want to give to God first because of your love for him and the things of God. Secondly, you want to consider the fact that you may have setup automatic draft payments of your mortgage, car notes, and other obligations to get drafted from your pay and we don't want to tithe off of what's left. We want to make God a priority and give to the kingdom of God first.

5% of the 100% - Give to Charitable Organizations

The **5%** offering is for giving an offering on the week that you don't get paid and to other churches or charitable concepts. Try to make it a practice to be a blessing to a young child, an elderly or the man/woman of God as the Lord lead and guide you.

5% of the 100% - FUN!

The **5%** fun is for things that you want to do for yourself as you exercise discipline in your finances. This is so that you won't get faint and grow weary in well doing. So you can use this money in a fun way. Maybe you have a hobby that you want to eventually turn into a business, or take advantage of a big ticket item you want to pay with cash, or take a nice exotic vacation. You can use this money for that.

10% of the 100% - Savings

The **10%** savings will help you move towards having a minimum of 8 months of income saved as emergency funds just in case you get laid off or hospitalized, etc. This money will be used to take care of your monthly expenses to help you avoid accumulating late fees or 30 day no pays reported on your credit report. Once you have your emergency funds account funded, you can then start funding your short and long term savings account.

70% of the 100% - Expenses

The **70%** should be the total of all of your expenses. The ideal number we want to strive for is 50% expenses so that you can use the other 20% for long term investments. In another training, we will discuss the various expenses and how to put together a strategy to eliminate unnecessary expenses.

Once you are done populating your Monthly Cashflow Statement, you will have a true picture of how your money is being spent on a monthly basis. It doesn't matter how bad it may look, you have done the natural now watch God do the supernatural. As you take this **Monthly Cashflow Statement** to God during your time of prayer, God will begin to download kingdom instructions pertaining to your financial situation. You will then need to have faith, trust God and implement whatever strategies he instructs you to execute.

Now don't get disgusted or frustrated when doing this because remember, Philippians 4:13 which says, *"I can do all things through Christ which strengthens me."*

PART 2: TRACK DAILY SPENDING

Once you have written down everything you need to pay on your Monthly Cashflow Statement, you will write down the amount of money left over to live off until your next pay day on your **Track It! Slips**. These slips can be ordered by visiting http://trackitslips.com. This is done so that you won't overspend and you can see where you are spending your money daily as you swipe your debit/credit card or get cash from an ATM.

Track It! Slips will help you ...

· Discover how much money you're *really* spending on lunch weekly

· Discover what you *really* did with the cash you withdrew from the ATM

· Discover the balance you *really* have left on your gift card

DO YOU....

❖ Ever wonder why it seems as if you don't have enough money from paycheck to paycheck while you're spending most of it on going out to lunch everyday?

❖ Ever get frustrated when you try to use a gift card that you know has a balance but gets denied anyway since you don't know the exact balance?

❖ Get worried because you can't figure out what you did with the money you know you withdrew from the ATM?

Well, I would like to put an end to these mind boggling situations and put you on the track of discovering what's really going on. I would like to introduce to you the **Track It! Slips** concept that will help to ease your mind and put you in more control of your everyday financial transactions. This can be done by using the Track It! Slips.

You and your family members can use the Track It! Slips every time you go out to lunch, withdraw money from the ATM or receive a gift card. Once you start using the Track It! Slips, you will begin to see where you are spending your money and begin to make minor adjustments to get your desired result which is to have more money.

GUESS WHAT?

The money is already there. So, get started on the road to discovery and watch yourself move from operating in a vicious cycle of wondering, worrying and frustration to operating in a victorious cycle of increase, abundance and overflow. Each booklet contains 25 slips for tracking daily spending, ATM withdrawals and Gift Card balances. These slips can easily be placed in your existing wallet along with your  debit/credit card. So slip one into your purse, his wallet and/or a child's backpack.

Now I also want you to know that I am aware that this is the technology era and there's an app for everything. But, I want you to rediscover the power of a pen and paper as you journey into creating financial success. So you can download an app to track your daily spending if that works better for you or you can write down your spending on these slips, it's your choice; but, please do resolve that you will implement this practice with your daily spending.

Now we will delve into tracking your monthly expenses in details.

PART 3: 30 DAY EXPENSE TRACKING FORM

After you have determined the total amount of monthly expenses and want to work on a strategy to lower them, download the 30 day expense tracking form. Make as many copies as needed so that each day for 30 days, you can write down every expense.
Download link => http://tjandtjinsuranceagency/expensetracking

After the 30 days, we will meet with you online or in person to evaluate your findings and determine where you can make adjustments to accomplish your financial goal. I will go into depth with the expense tracking strategy in another training session.

PART 4: PERSONAL FINANCES OVERVIEW

Print the personal finances overview form provided in this training. At the start of each quarter, prepare a personal finances overview so you will have an overview of your financial portfolio that will reflect what you have and what you owe.

CONCLUSION: I pray that this information was empowering, enlightening and motivating. If you are already a 90/10 steward then praise the Lord. If you aren't, I pray that you will spend time with God in prayer about being a 90/10 steward so that you can be a blessing to the kingdom of God as an end time financier.

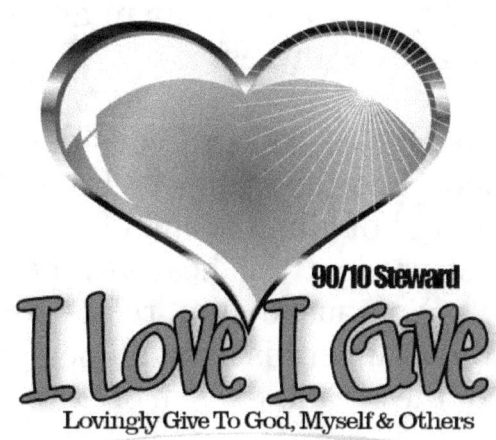

90/10 Steward

I Love I Give

Lovingly Give To God, Myself & Others

SCRIPTURE MEDITATION

Here are some scriptures to meditate on as you implement spiritual financial wisdom.

John 3:16 - For God so loved the world that he gave his only begotten son that whosoever believeth in him should not perish but have everlasting life.

Malachi 3:10-12 - Bring ye all the tithes into the storehouse that there may be meat in my house and prove me now herewith saith the Lord of host if I will not open you the windows of heaven and pour you out a blessing that there shall not be room enough to receive it. And I will rebuke the devourer for your sakes and he shall not destroy the fruits of your ground neither shall your vine cast her fruit before the time in the field saith the Lord of host. And all nations shall call you blessed for ye shall be a delightsome land saith the Lord of host.

Luke 12:42 - And the Lord said, who then is that faithful and wise steward, whom his Lord shall make ruler over his household, to give them their portion of meat in due season?

Genesis 8:22 - While the earth remaineth, seed time and harvest, cold and heat and summer and winter and day and night shall not cease.

Matthew 22:37-39 - Jesus said unto him, thou shalt love the Lord thy god with all thy heart and with all thy soul and with all your mind. This is the first and great commandment and the second is like unto it thou shalt love thy neighbor as thyself.

Psalms 8:3-8 - When I consider your heavens, the work of your fingers, the moon and the stars which you have set in place what is man that you are mindful of him, the son of man that you care for him. You made him a little lower than the heavenly beings and crowned him with glory and honor. You made him ruler over the works of your hands, you put everything under his feet all flock and herbs and the beasts of the field, the birds of the air and the fish of the sea all that swim the paths of the seas.

Joshua 1:8 - This book of the law shall not depart out of thy mouth; but thou shalt meditate therein day and night, that thou mayest observe to do according to all that is written therein: for then thou shalt make thy way prosperous, and then thou shalt have good success.

Deuteronomy 8:18 - But thou shalt remember the LORD thy God: for it is he that giveth thee power to get wealth, that he may establish his covenant which he sware unto thy fathers, as it is this day.

Proverbs 3:9-10 - Honour the LORD with thy substance, and with the firstfruits of all thine increase: So shall thy barns be filled with plenty, and thy presses shall burst out with new wine.

Galatians 3:29 - And if ye be Christ's, then are ye Abraham's seed, and heirs according to the promise.

Psalms 34:8 - O taste and see that the LORD is good: blessed is the man that trusteth in him.

I know we covered a lot in this chapter but it will help you get everything setup properly. I want to thank you for giving me the opportunity to minister to you in the area of kingdom finances. I pray that as you walk in obedience, implement financial disciplines and trust God, you will have a testimony of how God moved in your finances supernaturally!

Training Takeaways:

1. Love God, yourself and others
2. Tithe 10%
3. Be a good steward with the remaining 90% because all of it belongs to God.
4. Start a budget using the Monthly Cashflow Statement
5. Start tracking your daily expenses for 30 days
6. Determine net worth using the Personal Finances Overview Form
7. Increase your faith and trust in God by meditating of the Word of God

MONTHLY CASHFLOW STATEMENT

1st PAYDAY GROSS = _____ 2nd PAYDAY GROSS= _____

NET PAY = _____ NET PAY =_____

10% TITHES _____ 10% TITHES _____

5% OFFERINGS _____ 5% OFFERINGS _____

5% FUN _____ 5% FUN _____

10% SAVINGS _____ 10% SAVINGS _____

70% LIVING EXPENSE   70% LIVING EXPENSE

Rent/Mortgage $ _____ % _____   Rent/Mortgage $ _____ % _____

Lights/Electricity $ _____ % _____   Lights/Electricity $ _____ % _____

Water $ _____ % _____   Water $ _____ % _____

Cable $ _____ % _____   Cable $ _____ % _____

Phone $ _____ % _____   Phone $ _____ % _____

Car Insurance $ _____ % _____   Car Insurance $ _____ % _____

Car Fuel $ _____ % _____   Car Fuel $ _____ % _____

Food $ _____ % _____   Food _____ % _____

Credit Card $ _____ % _____   Credit Card $ _____ % _____

Other $ _____ % _____   Other $ _____ % _____

TOTAL $ _____ % _____ TOTAL $ _____ % _____

MONTHLY CASHFLOW STATEMENT (Example)

1st PAYDAY GROSS = _$2500____ 2nd PAYDAY GROSS= _$2500_____

NET PAY = _____$1789____ NET PAY =_____$1789_____

10% TITHES _____$250____ 10% TITHES _____$250_____

5% OFFERINGS _____$89_____ 5% OFFERINGS _____$89_____

5% FUN _____$89_____ 5% FUN _____$89_____

10% SAVINGS _____$179_____ 10% SAVINGS _____$179____

70% LIVING EXPENSE   70% LIVING EXPENSE

Rent/Mortgage $ _____400_____%_____   Rent/Mortgage $ _____400_____%_____

Lights/Electricity $____125____%_____   Lights/Electricity $ _____%_____

Water $_____50____%_____   Water $ _____%_____

Cable $ _____%_____   Cable $ _____60____%_____

Phone $_____%_____   Phone $ _____65____%_____

Car Insurance $ _____%_____   Car Insurance $_____88____%_____

Car Fuel $ _____100_____%_____   Car Fuel $_____100____%_____

Food $ _____100_____%_____   Food _____100___%_____

Credit Card $ _____35_____%_____   Credit Card $_____35____%_____

Other $_____%_____   Other $_____%_____

TOTAL $ _____810_____%_____   TOTAL $ _____848__%_____

For the Month of: _____

30-Day Expense Tracking Form   (From Spendable Income)

Week 1	Week 2	Week 3	Week 4	Total

Offerings & Other Seed Sowing
church, ministries, charities

_____ _____ _____   _____ _____

Housing
mortgage, rent, insurance

_____ _____ _____   _____ _____

maintenance, cleaning supplies, utilities, phone, cable, property taxes

_____ _____ _____   _____ _____

Food
groceries, lunch money, snacks, coffee

_____ _____ _____   _____ _____

Clothing/Shoes
new purchases, dry cleaning, laundry, tailor

_____ _____ _____   _____ _____

Transportation
car payments, bus, train, taxi, parking, gas
maintenance, repairs, insurance, taxes, license

_____ _____ _____   _____ _____

Insurance
health, life, dental, property, other

_____ _____ _____   _____ _____

Medical Expenses
doctor, Rx, dentist eye glasses, fitness

————— ————— ————— ————— —————

Child Care/School Expenses
daycare, tuition, allowance, child support, alimony

————— ————— ————— ————— —————

Outstanding Debt
credit cards, personal bank loans , family loans, 401K loans, etc.

————— ————— ————— ————— —————

Personal Grooming
toiletries, barber and beauty shop, nails, spas

————— ————— ————— ————— —————

Savings & Investments
contingency, retirement/401k, college, real estate

————— ————— ————— ————— —————

Entertainment/Recreation
dining out, vacation, hobbies, movies, other

————— ————— ————— ————— —————

Pet Care
pet food, grooming, veterinarian, insurance

————— ————— ————— ————— —————

Miscellaneous
gifts, birthdays, anniversaries, magazines, other

————— ————— ————— ————— —————

Total Amount Spent

————— ————— ————— ————— —————

PERSONAL FINANCES OVERVIEW

ASSETS
Liquid Assets _____

Cash _____

Mortgages _____

Checking Account _____

Savings Account _____

Total Assets $ _____

LIABILITIES
Car Loans _____

Bank Loans _____

Student Loans _____

Home Equity Loans _____

Other Loans _____

Credit Card Balances _____

Property Taxes Owed _____

Total Liabilities $ _____

INVESTED ASSETS
401K Plans _____

Real Estate _____

Certificates of Deposits _____

Stocks & Bonds _____

Mutual Funds _____

PERSONAL USE ASSETS
Home _____

Cars _____

Jewelry _____

Collectables _____

Furnishings _____

NET WORTH (assets - liabilities) $_____

3 JESUS WAS ON A MISSION, ARE YOU?

SCRIPTURE: **Luke 4:18-19** *"The Spirit of the Lord is upon me, because He hath anointed me to preach the gospel to the poor; he hath sent me to heal the broken hearted, to preach deliverance to the captives and recovery of sight to the blind, to set at liberty them that are bruised, to preach the acceptable year of the Lord."*

TOPIC: Jesus Was On A Mission, Are You?

PRAYER: Dear Heavenly Father, thank you for this day, thank you for being our Lord and Saviour. Thank you for using us, choosing us and placing us in your kingdom for such a time as this. As we study the mission of our Heavenly Father, I pray that you will empower us with your Holy Spirit to do the things that we are already predestined and purposed to do for your glory. Give us wisdom, knowledge and understanding that only comes from you. I pray that as we set out to do your good and perfect will for our lives that we would bring about a change in not only our lives but the lives of others also. Help us to be good stewards over everything you have placed in our possession. Let us take dominion, subdue, multiply, replenish and be fruitful. In Jesus Name Amen.

REVIEW: Now in the previous two chapters, our teaching was on the 3 key foundational strategies of The 90/10 Steward, I Love Therefore I Give and the components of the **Monthly Cashflow Statement**. In this chapter we are going to continue by covering the next concept which is our mission statement in relation to being a 90/10 Steward.

But before we do that, let's review what a 90/10 steward is:

A 90/10 steward is "a Christian who loves the Lord, has spiritual wisdom as well as practical financial wisdom." This love is evident by reciprocating the same love given to us back to God, you and others. The spiritual wisdom is evident by a Christian operating in obedience to the Word of God with their finances. The practical financial wisdom is evident by implementing discipline with their finances.	The 90/10 steward is tithing 10% of their income in obedience to Malachi 3:10 and they are also being a good steward over the 90% based on Luke 12:42. All of this is driven by the love that we have for God, ourselves and others in line with John 3:16.

Then we also looked at the definition of the word **steward** according to the Random House dictionary, which says that a steward is "**a person who manages another's property or financial affairs who administers anything as an agent for others.**"

So as a 90/10 steward, we are to implement spiritual wisdom as well as practical wisdom in obedience and with discipline over the whole 100% because it all belongs to God.

Now the last thing we will review from the previous teaching is the assignment. Your assignment was to create a Monthly Cashflow Statement. In order for us to lay the foundation necessary to become a 90/10 steward, the Monthly Cashflow Statement must be in place. And I believe that as you operated in obedience in creating your statement, you were richly rewarded by the Holy Spirit.

The last thing that I said as I ended the previous chapter was "I pray that as you walk in obedience, implement financial disciplines and trust God, you will have a testimony of how God moved in your finances supernaturally." Well guess what? I have a praise report of how God moved supernaturally in our finances because of walking in obedience and I look forward to hearing about yours.

TESTIMONY: Here is one of our testimonies. We have several properties that we purchased earlier in the year. At the end of the year, the taxes are due on those properties. These are extra expenses. This is what God did for us during the month the taxes were due: He supernaturally had my husband to receive a phone call from upper management on his job. He offered him a promotion to a job that other qualified candidates applied for but not my husband. My husband accepted the promotion. Now this promotion afford us the money to pay the taxes due on the property. Not only will this increase in salary cover the expenses for the taxes on the properties, but we will also have extra income every month. I believe the Lord blessed us with this promotion supernaturally for walking in obedience to His word.

So yes, **walking in obedience is rewarding**. You too can walk in expectancy and trust God will position you to give a testimony of something that was done supernaturally as well. Now you may or may not have a promotion to report and you may or may not be able to tell me of your praise report in person, but you can tell your neighbor, your friend or someone you are near. Now let's give God some praise for what He has done. Halleluah, Thank You Jesus – Oh bless His Holy Name.

ON A MISSION: Now, let's delve into our training, Jesus was on a mission, are you?

The definition of the word **mission** according to the Merriam Webster Dictionary – "mission is **a pre-established and often self-imposed objective or purpose.**" Pre-established meaning something that you have decided within yourself that you are going to do and self-imposed objective meaning you are going to do everything necessary to accomplish what you have decided to do.

So as we set out to become a 90/10 steward with our finances, we need to look at our motivator which is our mission. Ask yourself, what is it that motivates me to be a 90/10 steward over my finances? In other words, what is it that you are trying to accomplish financially overall?

Before you can determine what motivates you, you must spend time in prayer with God and maybe even fast in order for you to be prepared to be a 90/10 steward. As you spend time with God in prayer, you will get revelation from him so that you will know what your purpose is in the kingdom of God in the area of finances in order to be an end time financier.

As you bring your own personal goals and desires before God, He will show you any plans or goals that you may have that may not be his will for your life. Lastly, you will be strengthened and empowered by the Holy Spirit to implement the discipline necessary to implement his plan for your life with your finances to be a 90/10 steward and end time financier.

This is what Jesus did – he spent time in prayer and fasted in order for Him to boldly proclaim his mission which is outlined in our scripture for today which is Luke 4:17-18 which reads ***"The Spirit of the Lord is upon me, because He hath anointed me to preach the gospel to the poor; he hath sent me to heal the broken hearted, to preach deliverance to the captives and recovery of sight to the blind, to*** *set at liberty them that are bruised, to preach the acceptable year of the Lord."*

So there is no question about what he was sent here to do. Not only did he know what his mission was but he also fulfilled his mission because "faith without works is dead." (**James 2:14 KJV**) There are numerous accounts of miracles performed by Jesus through the books of Matthew, Mark, Luke and John.

You will be equipped to operate in the same boldness and power after you have spent time with the Lord and filled with the Holy Spirit to get directions and strategies in the area of finances. You too will be able to walk in obedience by tithing 10% and implementing discipline with the 90% so that the mission that Jesus had can continue to be your mission and your motivator.

Just think about this, if we don't tithe:

- How can the gospel continue to be preached to the poor?
- Where will the broken hearted go if the church isn't able to stay open because the church funds are depleted.
- How can those who are held captive by the enemy in all kinds of perversions be loosed if they aren't able to come to the house of God to hear a word that will set them free?
- How will those who have been blinded by this world's way of doing things have their eyes opened to God's way of doing things if the church doesn't exist?
- How can those who have been bruised by the enemy know that God still loves them and have a wonderful plan for their life if the church is not available?
- And how can those who have been living a life of sin and shame come to know that they can repent and be accepted into the kingdom of God.

Now you may be asking what does this have to do with tithing? It has everything to do with it. We are on a mission. We are in this world but not of this world. We are ambassadors for Christ. We are here to be fruitful, to multiply, replenish subdue and dominate. We have been anointed and placed in the kingdom for such a time of this.

The question was posed in **Luke 18:8**, "when the Son of man cometh shall he find faith on the earth?" The Bible says that in the last days there will be famines, wars and perilous times. Despite these things, our Heavenly Father wants to know if He can count you, can He count on you to continue to be faithful in tithing and not lose hope, get faint or grow weary in well doing.

God is definitely faithful to His Word and promises; but the problem arises when His people become discouraged; will not **continue to pray**; will not **continue to put trust in him**; and will, under heavy trials, test and

tribulations sink into despair. Don't you want to please God, don't you want to pleasure Him? Did you not say that you love him? Well, let love be your motivator to overcome all of these adversities and remain faithful.

Most of us have experienced love in the natural at some point in life. So if you can look at that love relationship, you will discover that when you love somebody you are looking to please them. You spend money on them and you not only tell them that you love them but you show them. You spend quality time with them and your money on them as well.

You subconsciously think about things you could do to keep this love thing going as long as possible. And as women I don't know if this is the case for a man but, as soon as a man starts cutting back on spending money on you, you start doubting his love for you and determine that he must be in love with somebody else and spending money on them since he isn't spending it on you. You begin to get jealous and start looking for clues of some other love affair.

In **Exodus 20:5** we see that God is the same way, he said he is a jealous God and he doesn't want you to have no other god besides him. He doesn't want you to take what belongs to him which is the tithe and give it to your

mortgage company or your cable service or your cell phone provider just because the economy is slow, or you have lost your job. In other words, he wants you to put your time, talent and your treasures into him through **fulfilling your mission and purpose** that he has revealed to you.

What's really your motivator here, paying your cable bill so that you can continue to watch "Who Wants to be A Millionaire" or is your motivator paying your tithe so that God can continue to open up the windows of heaven and pour you out a blessing so that you can become a millionaire yourself.

God is our heavenly father and he is so generous in his giving that he not only gave his only begotten son so that we can have a full life and an abundant life but he daily loads us with benefits. It's like waking up every morning to some long stems roses from your spouse or a card that says **I'm thinking about you** or here's a front row seat ticket to see your favorite football team play.

As your spouse "wow" you with various gestures, you in turn want to do the same gesture. As you walk in obedience in tithing, you will be perpetually showered with blessings such as goodness and mercy, protection, peace, good health and long life just to name a few. Just those few things alone should motivate you to walk in obedience and implement discipline in your finances. Jesus is looking to show himself mighty through you as you walk in obedience.

Now I'm going to point out some things that should **not** be your motivator – Your motivator should not be:

- I'm going to tithe and implement discipline because as I earn money I will be perceived as a successful person in the eyes of everybody
- As my finances increases, it is going to make me a happier person
- I won't have any worries since I will be able to take care of myself financially
- I think it will help me to get into good relationships with people that I have been trying to get into their circle

- It will get me anything my heart desires – I can buy that house I want now, I can buy that car I want now, etc.

These all are motivators that stem from the lust of the flesh, the lust of the eyes and the pride of life.

And when Jesus was tempted by satan with such desires, he stood on the Word and told satan what was written. And since you have been born again and empowered by the Holy Ghost, you too will be able to do the same thing. **Romans 8:35** says *"who shall separate us from the love of Christ? Shall tribulation, or distress or persecution or famine or nakedness or peril or sword?"*

So are you ready to get started working on your mission? I hope so. In order to do this, I want you to spend time in prayer with God and meditate on **Luke 4:17-18** to get revelation.

As you hear from God, He will reveal to you your passion. This will be your cause, your driving force, your motivation for tithing. You then will be able to devise your own mission statement based on your passion.

My passion is doing my part in the body of Christ by bringing my 10% to the house of God. It will go in with everybody else 10% so that we all can live the life that God has already predestined and purposed us to live. As children of the most High God, we will be a witness to those who will come into the house of God and don't believe that God takes care of his people. We will have the resources to go into communities and build houses, clothe the naked, feed the hunger, break generational curses and so much more. This will be the fruit of our labor as we come together on one accord in giving.

MISSION STATEMENT EXAMPLE

My mission statement is to enlighten and empower others to implement disciplines to be a 90/10 steward as end time financiers. In order for me to carry out this mission, I need to already be tithing, and already exercising spiritual and financial discipline in my own life. As I reflect on Luke 4:17-18, I can see where my tithing and giving is making a difference in the lives of individuals living from paycheck to paycheck. As they implement these financial disciplines, they too will begin to tithe and give offerings so there is meat in the storehouse according to Malachi 3:10. Not only will their needs be met but those who encounter us will begin to see that God takes care of his people.

So what's your motivator?

- Are you concerned about the poor?
- Are you compassionate about the disabled?
- Do you want to make a difference in the lives of those who have been misused and abused?
- Do you want to help empower disadvantaged youth?

What is the thing that gets you stirred in your spirit? Once you do this fact finding, you can begin to give passionately and see God work miracles, signs and wonders in not only your life but in the lives of others as well.

Remember, this is not about you. Jesus gave us 2 commandments in **Mark 12:30-31** and I'm paraphrasing here – but the first one is to love the Lord with all your heart, mind, soul and strength and the second one is to love your neighbor as yourself.

CONCLUSION: Let's have a vibrant healthy love life with God since it is harvest time and the church doors need to be open. There are many people in the valley of decision and they need to have a place to come to grow in the Lord once they decide to live for Jesus. As we operate as a 90/10 steward, then our love will be put in action and felt. Let the church feel your love so that it can continue to minister to the poor, lost, hurting, sick and bound.

SECOND ASSIGNMENT: The last thing to cover in this chapter is your assignment. You will devise a **Mission Statement** in line with the mission of our Lord and Saviour Jesus Christ as outlined in **Luke 4:17-18**.

I'M MOTIVATED!

MY MISSION STATEMENT

NAME: _____

Luke 4:17-18 "The Spirit of the Lord is upon me, because He hath anointed me to preach the gospel to the poor; he hath sent me to heal the broken hearted, to preach deliverance to the captives and recovery of sight to the blind, to set at liberty them that are bruised, to preach the acceptable year of the Lord."

For the poor:

_____
_____
_____

For the broken hearted:

_____
_____
_____

For the captives:

_____
_____
_____

For the blind:

_____
_____
_____

For the bruised:

_____
_____
_____

4 CONTENTMENT PLUS DILIGENCE EQUALS AN INCREASED CASHFLOW

SCRIPTURE: *Hebrews 13:5* *"Let your conversation be without covetousness; and be content with such things as ye have for He hath said I will never leave thee nor forsake thee."*

TOPIC: Contentment plus Diligence equals an Increased Cashflow

PRAYER: Dear Heavenly Father, thank you for this day, thank you for being our Lord and Saviour. Thank you for using us and choosing us and placing us in your kingdom for such a time as this. I pray that you will empower us with your Holy Spirit to be content with what you have already blessed us with. Help us to be diligent in implementing biblical wisdom with our finances so that we can do the things that we are already predestined and purposed to do for your glory. In Jesus name, Amen.

REVIEW: In the previous chapter, we continued building on the concepts of the The 90/10 Steward, I Love Therefore I Give. Your assignment was to devise a **Mission Statement** based on the mission Jesus had for the kingdom in relation to Luke 4:17-18. In this chapter we will go over the Monthly Cashflow Statement with concentration on the components of the 70% which is your expenses in details.

CONTENTMENT: Now based on our topic Contentment plus Diligence equals an Increased Cashflow, let's look at the definition of the word contentment according to Webster. **Contentment** is to be mentally and emotionally satisfied with things as they are or peace of mind.

As we go to the word of God pertaining to contentment, we see that **I Timothy 6:6-8** says *"Godliness with contentment is great gain. For we brought nothing into this world and it is certain we can carry nothing out. And having food and raiment let us be therewith content."* So let's look at three things we should be content with that are in our possession.

CLOTHES: This statement may sound simple but, "you have clothes to wear". Some people even have clothes categorized as church clothes, work clothes, hanging around the house clothes, special occasion clothes, etc.

FOOD: You have food to eat even if it isn't what you want to eat. Now, if you get tired of eating the same thing, look at some cookbooks and create a meal. Actually this may even payoff if you come up with a meal and submit it to some of the companies such as Pillsbury and Betty Crocker and win cash for your idea.

SHELTER: You also have somewhere to lay your head at night. Now you may be renting that place or you may still live at home with your parents. Regardless, at least you aren't living on the streets, under a bridge or sleeping on a parked bench.

Let's look at the contentment modeled by Jesus as He diligently set out to fulfill his mission. **Matthew 8:19-20** says *"and a certain scribe came and* *said unto him master, I will follow thee withersoever thou goest and Jesus said unto him, foxes have holes and the birds of the air have nests but the Son of man hath no where to lay his head."* In other words, if you are consumed with the things of this world more than the kingdom of God, then being a follower of Christ might become difficult.

There are many of us who may say "Lord use me" or "any way you bless me Lord I'll be satisfied" but do we really mean it?

DILIGENCE: Let's take a look at the definition of the word diligence according to Webster. Diligence is **"persistent personal attention, the attention or care legally expected or required of a person."**

As we look at the word diligent in the word of God we find **Joshua 22:5** which says "But take diligent heed to do the commandment and the law which Moses the servant of the Lord charged you to love the Lord your God and to walk in all his ways and to keep his commandments and to cleave unto him and to serve him with all your heart and with all your soul." So when you operate as a 90/10 steward you are heeding to the commandment of the almighty God and proving your love towards him and that is when the windows of heaven opens up over you. Let's look at some scriptures on being diligent.

Proverbs 10:4 – "He becometh poor that dealeth with a slack hand, but the hand of the diligent maketh rich." In other words, being lazy and not wanting to buckle down and create your Monthly Cashflow Statement will not get you the riches that God has in store for you.

Proverbs 10:5 – "He that gathered in summer is a wise son but he that sleepeth in harvest is a son that causeth shame." So we don't want to bring shame on the kingdom of God during economic crisis in the world by not creating a Monthly Cashflow Statement and not knowing where adjustments or modifications need to be made so that you, your family and your church can continue to function during economic crisis.

Proverbs 13:4 – "The sluggard craves and gets nothing but the desires of the diligent are fully satisfied." Here again laziness is unacceptable in the kingdom of God. You can't just mentally want to be a blessing to the kingdom financially. You must diligently do the things necessary so that when the church has a need, you will be able to step up to the plate and not feel like the church is infringing on you because of your lack of diligence.

Proverbs 21:5 - "The plans of the **diligent lead to profit** as surely as **haste leads to poverty**." So here we see that when we sit down and plan out our Monthly Cashflow Statement, we will profit. Not only will we profit individually but those connected to us will benefit also - our church, our children and our children's children.

As we strive to become a 90/10 steward we want to do our due diligence and look at every expense that we have to make sure that we are utilizing our finances at its most optimal use.

DUE DILIGENCE: The definition of due diligence according to Webster is "**the care that a reasonable person exercises to avoid unnecessary harm to either party involved in a transaction.**"

As contracts are signed to obtain financing for mortgages, rental property, cars, household items, etc. we need to keep in mind that we don't want to cause any unnecessary harm to either party involved in those transactions. In other words, we don't want to "not" pay the lender back their money and have bill collectors calling or have our credit score lowered. The newest way that having bad debt and credit is having an effect on people is in the job hiring process. There are some places of employment that will not hire you if you have bad credit. So keep that in mind when you make a decision to purchase items on credit.

CASHFLOW: Cashflow is **the money that you earn or are given that you use to conduct business.** Now you will see how well you have done with your finances in black and white as you fill in the blanks of your **Monthly Cashflow Statement.** You will now be empowered to proactively know where your cash is spent and make adjustments as needed. You will control the flow of your cash instead of your cash controlling the flow of you. You never want your cash to dictate what you can or cannot do, because **Deuteronomy 8:18** says "But thou shall remember the Lord thy God for it is he that giveth thee power to get wealth that he may establish his covenant which he sware unto thy fathers as it is this day."

As you operate in the power given to you by God, your contentment plus your diligence will result in an increased cashflow. Why increased? Because God says so - remember the 90/10 steward is all about love - it is never about you, but what God wants to do through you. Having this type of attitude towards your cashflow is why "your barns will be full to overflowing and your vats will brim over" according to **Proverbs 3:10**. This also is why you will live a life of abundance according to **Ephesians 3:20.**

Your finances will be "pressed down shaken together and running over" according to **Luke 6:38**. Your little will become much and you will experience the supernatural like the multitude did when Jesus took 2 fish and five loaves and fed them according to **Luke 9:16-17**. God wants to sow into you so that you can be used in the area of finances for the end time harvest of souls for the kingdom of God. All you have to do is what you know to do in the natural and God will do the supernatural.

You are going to have to do what was done in **Haggai 2:2** which says "Write the vision and make it plain so that those who read it can run with it." So as we write out our expenses as a starting point, we then will go to God for revelation and direction on where adjustments can be made so that we can know without a doubt that we are in the will of God. God is going to remove the blinders so that when you are done looking at your expenses, you will see them in a whole new light.

Yes it is going to take discipline but just like you have conditioned yourself to do what you are doing now, you can modify your actions through the power of the almighty God and walk in victory with your finances.

EXPENSES: Now let's talk about the components of the expenses. This information is a culmination of several financial resources since I wanted to make sure that I covered every expense possible. I'll categorize these as food, shelter, clothing, transportation and others.

Food Category: Food expenses are groceries, lunch money, snacks, breakfast money, dining out – **5 to 15%** of your income can be allotted towards food.

Shelter Category: Shelter expenses are mortgage, rent, homeowner's insurance, renter's insurance, home owner's association dues, property taxes, electricity, water, gas, garbage removal, cable, internet, household supplies, repairs/maintenance, improvements, furnishings such as draperies, bedding, paintings – **25 to 40%** of your income can be allotted towards shelter.

Clothing Category: Clothing expenses are uniforms, casual clothing, business clothing, purses, shoes, children's clothing, hats, coats, dry cleaning, laundry – **2 to 7%** of your income can be allotted towards clothing.

Personal Grooming Category: Personal grooming expenses are perms, cuts, manicures, spas, gyms, perfumes, colognes – **2 to 5%** of your income can be allotted towards personal grooming.

Transportation Category: Transportation expenses are car payment, bus pass, train, taxi, parking, tolls, gas, maintenance, repairs, insurance, taxes, license, boat, motorcycle, rv payment, storage fees – **5 to 15%** of your income can be allotted towards transportation.

Outstanding Debt or Credit Category: Outstanding debt or credit expenses are credit card payments, personal bank loans, family loans, 401k loans – **5 to 10%** of your income can be allotted towards outstanding debt.

Insurance Category: Insurance expenses are health, life, dental – 2 to 7% of your income can be allotted towards insurance.

Medical/Dental/Optical Category: Medical/dental/optical expenses are doctor visit co pay, Rx, dental co pay, eye glasses, and/or contact lens, gyms, chiropractor, medical equipment – **5 to 15%** can be alloted towards medical/dental/optical.

Childcare/School Expenses Category: Childcare/school expenses are daycare, babysitter fees, tuition, books, allowance, child support, alimony – **5 to 15%** of your income can be allotted towards childcare/school.

Entertainment Category: Entertainment expenses are vacations, birthday parties, magazine subscriptions, anniversaries, music, sports, dance lessons, tutoring, movie theatres, season sports tickets, bowling – **4 to 7%** of your income can be allotted towards entertainment.

Pet Care Category: Pet care expenses are pet food, grooming, vet charges, insurance, toys – **2 to 4%** of your income can be allotted towards pet care.

CONCLUSION: Once you are done populating your Monthly Cashflow Statement, spend time with God in prayer and ask him for revelation to the strategy that will reduce your expenses to 50% of your overall income.

The reason you want to get revelation from the Holy Spirit on what to do is so that you will walk away with a plan of action knowing that the one who sits high and looks low has favored you to be apart of his divine plans to redeem man back to himself.

You are going to feel honored and a sense of duty knowing that there is no greater calling than to be chosen to be used by the Lord. You too will be known as a change agent, a history maker and a trendsetter. Think about the cloud of witnesses that have gone on before you that are cheering you on as the baton has been passed to you. Think about the impact you are going to make on the next generation as you leave a legacy of being a 90/10 steward for the kingdom of God.

THIRD ASSIGNMENT: The last thing to cover in this chapter is your assignment - **Keep Doing, Stop Doing, Start Doing Worksheet.** You will populate this worksheet with the following information:

- **First**: what are you doing that is working and that you need to keep doing.
- **Second**: what are you doing that is not working that you need to stop doing.
- **Third**: what things you need to start doing.

Ask the Lord for power to do all three so that you can become a 90/10 steward and an end time financier in order to reap the end time harvest of souls.

PRAYER: Heavenly Father, thank you for empowering us to be content. I pray that as we set out to do our due diligence with our finances that we would bring about a change in not only our lives but the lives of others also so that we can leave a legacy and an inheritance to our children's children. Help us to be good stewards over everything you have placed in our possession.　 Let us take dominion, subdue, multiply, replenish and be fruitful. In Jesus Name Amen.

KEEP DOING, STOP DOING, START DOING WORKSHEET

What are you doing that is working and you need to keep doing with your finances?

_____

_____

_____

_____

_____

_____

_____

What are you doing that is not working you need to stop doing with your finances?

_____

_____

_____

_____

_____

_____

_____

What things you need to start doing with your finances to meet your financial goals?

_____

_____

_____

_____

_____

_____

_____

5 I OWE YOU, NOT THEM

SCRIPTURE: **Romans 13:8** *"Owe no man anything but to love one another for he that loveth another hath fulfilled the law."*

TOPIC: I Owe You, Not Them

PRAYER: Dear Heavenly Father, thank you for empowering us through your word to become debt free. I pray that as you reveal to us that the only debt we should have is love for one another, help us to eliminate the debt that we have accumulated that we should not have. Forgive us and help us to implement these kingdom strategies and financial principles with our finances for your glory, Amen.

REVIEW: In the previous chapter, we reviewed the components of the Monthly Cashflow Statement expenses in details. In this chapter, we will go over the Creditor Debt Elimination Worksheet to position you to become debt free.

Before we discuss what needs to be done to become debt free, I want to say that I know that it took a lot of discipline to buckle down and create the Monthly Cashflow Statement and strategize a plan of action to reduce your monthly expenses. I pray that this will become a part of your monthly routine.

The concept behind creating the Monthly Cashflow Statement is key to your success in having your cash work for you instead of you working for cash – in other words, you will no longer live paycheck to paycheck and rob Peter to pay Paul. Now that you have created your Monthly Cashflow Statement, you can see where your money is spent and make adjustments accordingly.

The reason you will make adjustments accordingly is because some of the expenses that you have is debt that is hindering you from obtaining the wealth that God has already predestined for you to have. You have done great! You have written down all of your expenses and determined how much money you have left to spend after all your bills are paid. You will see how powerful and crucial of a role it will play in helping you achieve your goal of becoming debt free.

THE FIRST DEBT ELIMINATION IDEA

DEBT FREE: In this section. I will describe to you how to use some of your left over money to position you to become debt free. For those of you who don't have any money left over, I'm going to ask you to re-evaluate your Monthly Cashflow Statement. Look at your expenses and determine which one you can downsize or eliminate altogether. If you need help with this process, do not hesitate to contact us at tjandtjenterprise@gmail.com.

DEBT: Now let's look at the definition of debt to see why we want to be debt free. According to Merriam Webster dictionary, **debt is something owed, an obligation, sin, trespass**.

CREDITOR: In the financial arena the financial institution that money is borrowed from is referred to as a creditor. The definition of creditor is **one to whom a debt is owed especially a person to whom money or**

goods are due.

Let's look at some scriptures on debt and creditors to see the **consequences of having debt.**

Job 24:9 - The fatherless child is snatched from the breast, the infant of the poor is seized for a debt.

Matthew 18:23-25 - Therefore the kingdom of heaven is like a king who wanted to settle accounts with his servants, as he began the settlement a man who owed him ten thousand bags of gold was brought to him. Since he was not able to pay, the master ordered that he and his wife and his children and all that he had be sold to repay the debt.

II Kings 4:1: – The wife of a man from the company of the prophets cried out to Elisha, your servant my husband is dead and you know that he revered the Lord. But now his creditor is coming to take my two boys as his slaves.

Now based on our scripture for today **Romans 13:8** which says to *"Owe no man anything but to love one another for he that loveth another hath fulfilled the law,"* the only debt we should be responsible for is to love.

As we look back at the definition of debt, one of the words that described debt was sin. We all know that Jesus paid the price for our sin on the cross at Calvary. He who knew no sin became sin and we know that the wages of sin is death. So when Jesus died on the cross the payment of our sins was taken care of once and for all. Of course, this payment stemmed from the love the Heavenly Father has for us as his children. So let's follow his example of love when it comes to debt which means that we are to only owe love to one another.

Now I'm not saying that you won't have expenses, of course you will; but debt that prevents you from obtaining the wealth that you are entitled to is unacceptable and has serious penalties.

DEBT CASE STUDY

CASE STUDY: The scriptures we read earlier in this chapter described what happened to some of the people in the Bible during their era when a debt isn't paid back to a creditor based on the contractual agreement but let's take this to the 21st century.

One day a car buyer decided to borrow money from a creditor to purchase a vehicle. Not just any vehicle, but the one the buyer just had to have with all the bells and whistles too. Now the interest rate on this vehicle for the buyer was 3.9% because of the buyer's credit score. The buyer believed this to be a great rate.

Let's see what could potentially happen if the buyer ends up losing a job or something else happens so that the buyer isn't able to continue making the monthly payments:

1. The creditor will notify all three credit reporting services – Transunion, Equifax and Experian - of 30 days, 60 days or however many days late. When this is done, this will lower the buyer's credit score.
2. If too many months goes by without making any payments on the vehicle, the creditor will repossess the vehicle. This also will go on the buyer's credit report and lower the score.
3. Once the creditor sells the car and don't get back enough money to cover the amount of money borrowed, they then will still want the buyer to pay the remaining balance, if it not paid, then that balance will be turned over to a collection agency.
4. The collection agency will then call the buyer's mother, neighbor or anybody else that was put down as a personal reference to try to get payment of the remaining balance and embarrass the buyer at the same time.
5. They also will report to the credit reporting services if payment is not made to them. Now the original credit negative reporting is on the credit report, the repossession is on the report and then the collection agency negative reporting is on it also.
6. All of these negative transactions will be on the buyer's credit report

for 7 years.

7. If the buyer is looking for new employment, the buyer can be turned down for a job even if qualified because of a bad credit score. A bad credit score to employers is viewed as irresponsible behavior.

8. Lastly, if the buyer tries to buy another car after all this has taken place, the chances of getting a 3.9% interest rate will not be possible; instead, it may end up being double digits.

Now you might be wondering, how in the world do I know about this so well? Well, about 20 years ago, I co-signed for someone to get a car and the person didn't make the payments. So when I went to purchase a car, nobody wanted to loan me money because when they checked my credit, the repossession was on there.

Now personally I didn't have bad credit but when I co-signed for someone, it was just as if I borrowed the money myself. After going from car lot to car lot, I finally found a compassionate salesman that said he would take a chance on me and loan me the money to purchase a car.

The interest rate they charged me was **26%**. They said if I paid this without any late pays, this will get my credit back in good standings. So I borrowed the money for 2 years and paid as promised. Bottom line, do not co-sign unless you are willing to make payments for a loan you have co-signed on.

My suggestion for purchasing a car is that you determine first how much money you can afford to pay monthly as a car note. Once you decide that, save that amount of money for 2 years. For example, if you determined that you could afford a $400 car note that would mean at the end of 2 years, you would have saved $9,600.

You then can pay cash for a decent car at an auction or at a used car lot. This is just an example of how you can purchase a car and not create debt to do it. Keep in mind that a car is to get you from point a to point b. Also, a car is a depreciating asset. You want to stay away from that kind of debt.

If you want to purchase a more high end vehicle, just make sure that you do your due diligence and not get into debt by purchasing it to impress or make others think that you have more than what you really do. This also applies to the purchase of a house as well.

APPRECIATING VS DEPRECIATING: A house is an appreciating asset. The difference in depreciating assets and appreciating assets is that a depreciating asset loses its value the longer you have it and an appreciating asset increases its value the longer you have it.

If you purchase a house and cannot make the monthly payments on it, the creditor will foreclose on the house and put it on your credit report and it will stay on your report for 7 years also.

Before you decide to create debt, read **Deuteronomy 15:1-2 NIV** which says "*At the end of every seven years you must cancel debt*." So keep this in mind that any derogatory reporting on your credit report can remain on it up to 7 years.

HARM'S WAY: There are two major purchases that can put individuals in harm's way if the debt isn't paid back. So, I began to ponder on the thought, what is it that would make a person deliberately bring harm to themselves financially? There are three things that may contribute to this behavior:

1. The first may be that some people have not been taught how to budget and have a problem when someone tries to teach them anything pertaining to money. **Proverbs 11:14** says "*where no counsel is, the people fall, but in the multitude of counsellors, there is safety*." So attending workshops, buying books and studying the word on finances will help you to gain the knowledge needed to position you to receive the blessings of God and not curses.

2. The second may be that some people are mimicking what they have seen done by their parents. **Psalms. 78:8** says "*and might not be as their fathers a stubborn and rebellious generation, a generation that set not their heart aright and whose spirit was not stedfast with God*." Just because your parents weren't good stewards, it doesn't mean that you have to walk in those generational curses.

3. The third might occur because of simple acts of carnality, wanting to continue to be like the world and wanting everything we see that will make us feel good and look good to others. **I John 2:15-16** says *"love not the world neither the things that are in the world, If any man love the world, the love of the father is not in him. For all that is in the world, the lust of the flesh, the lust of the eyes and the pride of life is not of the Father but is of the world."*

Now don't get me wrong, it isn't that God does not want you to partake of everything that he has positioned you to have, the problem comes in when you love the things more than you love the things of God.

Deuteronomy. 11:28-29 says *"Behold I set before you this day, a blessing and a curse; a blessing, if you obey the commandments of the Lord your God which I command you this day; and a curse, if you will not obey the commandments of the Lord your God but turn aside out of the way which I command you this day to go after other gods which ye have not known."*

I don't know about you but I want my life to represent the blessings of the Lord.

CONCLUSION: Here is what you should have on your Debt Elimination Worksheet:
A list of all creditors, your balance from your monthly statement, your minimum amount due from your monthly statement, the interest rate charged from your monthly statement, the amount that you actually paid your creditor for the month and the timeframe to pay it off by utilizing a financial calculator: http://www.bankrate.com/calculators.aspx.

Lastly, do the natural and watch God supernaturally make you debt free!

ASSIGNMENT: Now the last thing I want to cover with you is your assignment - the **Creditor Debt Elimination Worksheet**. You will use this Creditor Debt Elimination to become debt free.

In order to populate your Creditor Debt Elimination Worksheet, you will need your monthly statement from your creditor – make sure to review your creditor monthly statement for mistakes since they are computer generated. Make sure they reflect the right interest rate and payment information. Yearly contact your creditor in faith and ask for a reduction in your interest rate.

You will also need a financial calculator – this will be used to determine the timeframe it will take to pay off each creditor based on your outstanding balance and minimum payment due. If you don't own one, you can utilize the one on my website http://tjandtjenterprise.com/join or at http://www.bankrate.com/calculators.aspx.

Print a **Creditor Debt Elimination Worksheet** for each month. You will list the creditors and pay creditors based on the one that will be paid off in the least amount of time. This will help you to see immediate results and not get weary in well doing as you begin to implement your plan of action.

Implement this plan by paying the amount of debt that is listed in the column titled **Actual Paid** since this is the amount of debt you will be paying monthly.

Next, prioritize the payment of the creditors in this order: first list credit cards, furniture bills, line of credits with high interest rates, then car loans, then mortgage.

At first, the amount in the **Minimum Payment** column and the **Actual Paid** column will be the same. On your monthly statement from your creditor, you will have a minimum amount due. Use this as information only.

As you pay down your debt, your creditor will lower the minimum amount due. Do not lower the amount that you are paying to the new lowered minimum payment amount due from your statement. This has been lowered only to keep you in bondage. Continue to pay the amount listed in the Actual Paid column until the debt is paid in full.

You will need to ask God to reveal to you where you can scale back with your expenses in order to get an extra $25 or $50 to add to your Minimum Amount Due for your first creditor. Now depending on how much debt you owe, you may need to come up with a higher number. In any case, this will start the debt elimination process.

DEBT ELIMINATION EXAMPLE

Example: If your first creditor minimum payment is $25, you will actually pay them $50 or $75 depending on whether or not you will be able to add an extra $25 or $50 from your leftover expenses. You will then pay the $50 or $75 until the first creditor balance is paid in full.

Once you finish paying your first creditor, you will then take that $50 or $75 that you were paying to the first creditor and add it to the second creditor minimum payment. You will pay that new amount until your second creditor is paid in full. This is to be done for all creditors until you are debt free.

Lastly, pray that as you are successful in becoming debt free that you do not celebrate by getting back into debt. Instead be a blessing to the kingdom of God by sharing these principles to your children, your children's children and to others so they too can be empowered by God to be debt free as they implement kingdom strategies. You will be able to do this because you know now that you are to owe no man anything but to love them.

CREDITOR DEBT ELIMINATION (Example)

MONTH_____October_____DATE: ___10/1_____

I CAN DO ALL THINGS THROUGH CHRIST (PHILIPPIANS 4:13)

CREDITOR	BEG. BAL	MIN. PAYMENT	INT. RATE	ACTUALPAID	TIMEFRAME
JCPenney	1,185.00	35.00	17%	35.00+50.00 (extra) **$85.00**	16months instead of 47 months
Other Loan	$9,110.00	$350.00	12%	350.00+85.00 (extra) **$445.00**	24months instead of 31months
Mortgage	$159,212.00	$1059.00	7%	1059+445 (extra) **$1504.00**	16years instead of 30years

TOTAL:

	$169,507				

CREDITOR DEBT ELIMINATION

MONTH_____DATE: _____

I CAN DO ALL THINGS THROUGH CHRIST (PHILIPPIANS 4:13)

CREDITOR	BEG. BAL	MIN. PAYMENT	INT. RATE	ACTUALPAID	TIMEFRAME

TOTAL:

6 HERE'S HOW TO OBTAIN WEALTH

SCRIPTURE: **Exodus 31:1-5** *"Then the Lord said to Moses, see I have called by name Bezaleel, the son of Uri, the son of Hur, of the tribe of Judah, and I have filled him with the Spirit of God, with skill, ability and knowledge of all kinds of crafts – to make artistic designs for work in gold, silver and bronze, to cut and set stones, to work in wood and to engage in all kinds of craftsmanship."*

TOPIC: Here's How to Obtain Wealth

PRAYER: Dear Heavenly Father, thank you for this day, thank you for your Word that heals, delivers and sets free. Reveal to us on this day, the skills, ability and knowledge already given to us by you to obtain wealth for your glory, Amen.

REVIEW: Now in the previous chapter, we continued by going over the concepts from The 90/10 Steward, I Love Therefore I Give Workshop and we reviewed the **Creditor Debt Elimination Worksheet** which detailed the process to implement to get out of debt.

This month we will go over what it takes to obtain wealth to assist in the debt elimination process. This is one of my favorite topics since this subject propel us into creativity mode. I have heard the saying "in order to get a miracle, you need a miracle situation." Well, I believe that since you have decided to walk in faith to follow the debt elimination process, this act of obedience has positioned you to receive a miracle. So, thank the Lord in advance for what he is getting ready to do.

As discussed with the **Creditor Debt Elimination Worksheet**, the way you are to start your debt elimination process is to determine where you can cutback to have an extra $25, $50 or whatever amount you determined you need to start paying off your first creditor until all debt is eliminated. In this chapter, we will discuss in details the second way to assist in that process which is to obtain wealth as you **tap into your creativity** using your skills, knowledge and ability.

WEALTH: Let's look at the definition of **wealth** according to Merriam Webster – it is an abundance of valuable material possession or resources; an abundant supply; all property that has a money value or an exchangeable value.

As I did a word search in the Bible for the Word wealth, I saw that there were several illustrations where wealth was obtained and used to the glory of God and I also read some scriptures that illustrated what would happen to wealth if it is ill-gained or gotten with the wrong motive. Remember in a previous chapter, we talked about your mission which dealt with your passion for the things of God. If your motive for obtaining wealth is not derived from the love of God, the love of his people and the things pertaining to God, you will not have it very long. If your motive is right, you will be able to do what the first part of **Proverbs 13:22** says which is "A good man leaves an inheritance to his children's children"; if your motive isn't right, you will partake of the second part of this same verse which says "And the wealth of the sinner is laid up for the just."

God knows the heart and intent of the heart so you will not be able to fool God. **Luke 16:15** says "Ye are they which justify yourselves before men; but God knoweth your hearts; for that which is highly esteemed among men is an abomination in the sight of God."

Now let's look at some individuals in the Bible who obtained wealth because of having a right heart towards the things of God.

The first person is Jehoshaphat:

II Chronicles 17:3-6 NIV version says "The LORD was with Jehoshaphat because in his early years he walked in the ways his father David had followed. He did not consult the Baals but sought the God of his father and followed his commands rather than the practices of Israel." Now because of his heart towards the things of God, verse 5 says The LORD established the kingdom under his control; and all Judah brought gifts to Jehoshaphat, so that he had great wealth and honor. The reason this happened is because of verse 6 which says "His heart was devoted to the ways of the LORD; furthermore, he removed the high places and the Asherah poles from Judah." NIV

The second person is Solomon:

1 Kings 3:7-14 NIV version says "Now, O LORD my God, you have made your servant king in place of my father David. But I am only a little child and do not know how to carry out my duties. Your servant is here among the people you have chosen, a great people, too numerous to count or number. So give your servant a discerning heart to govern your people and to distinguish between right and wrong. For who is able to govern this great people of yours?" The Lord was pleased that Solomon had asked for this. So God said to him, "Since you have asked for this and not for long life or wealth for yourself, nor have asked for the death of your enemies but for discernment in administering justice, I will do what you have asked. I will give you a wise and discerning heart, so that there will never have been anyone like you, nor will there ever be."

Now look at how God rewards him for having the right motive in **verse 13** which says, "Moreover, I will give you what you have not asked for — both riches and honor — so that in your lifetime you will have no equal among kings. And if you walk in my ways and obey my statutes and commands as David your father did, I will give you a long life." NIV

The third person is Isaac:

Genesis 26:1-3 NIV version says "Now there was a famine in the land besides the earlier famine of Abraham's time and Isaac went to Abimelech King of the Philistines in Gerar. The Lord appeared to Isaac and said "do not go down to Egypt"; live in the land where I tell you to live. Stay in this land for a while and I will be with you and bless you. For to you and your descendants I will give all these lands and will confirm the oath I swore to your father Abraham."

Now let's skip down to **verse 12-14** to see what happened because of his obedience, it says "Isaac planted crops in that land and the same year reaped a hundredfold, because the LORD blessed him. The man became rich, and his wealth continued to grow until he became very wealthy. He had so many flocks and herds and servants that the Philistines envied him." So, are you ready to obtain the type of wealth that make others envy it? This is what can happen for you too.

Take note that these three scenarios were about what God had in mind for his people. It is never about the individual. God is always looking for someone to show himself mighty in as he establish His kingdom here on earth as it is in heaven.

Now that we understand that our obedience to God, our passion for the things of God and having the right motive positions us to receive wealth, let's look at how we have been wired up naturally to obtain it.

THE SECOND DEBT ELIMINATION IDEA

As we look at our scripture for today, we see that Bezaleel was filled by the spirit of God with knowledge, skills and abilities. Guess What? We all have been blessed with knowledge, skills and abilities. So, in order for you to obtain the wealth, you are going to need to assess your knowledge, skills and abilities.

These things coupled with the Holy Ghost will get you on the path to realizing what you are anointed to do to obtain wealth. Based on our scripture for today, Moses had an assignment so the Lord blessed him with someone that had the knowledge, skills and abilities Moses needed. So even if you don't know how to do what you have been assigned to do, God will favor you with the people who do.

When it comes to knowledge, skills and abilities, most of the time, others are able to pick up on the fact that you are gifted to do something before you do. The reason this happens is because normally it is something that you are already doing and love to do.

Not only are you great at operating in this gift and doing it, but you will do it for any one, at any time and whether or not you get a dime for doing it, you will still do it. You don't consider the cost or the time involved because it is what you were put on this earth to do. And when the question is asked amongst a crowd "who is a great resource" for what you do, your name is always the one referenced. Well guess what? That is where you have been gifted to obtain your wealth, your money anointing.

So if you are known for baking the best pies, cookies or cakes on this side of the world, I suggest you thank the Lord and start operating in your money anointing to generate residual income from it to the glory of God. So as you tap into your money anointing and start accumulating residual income, you can accelerate the process of becoming debt free.

The definition of **residual** according to Merriam Webster is – that which is leftover, additional pay given for reruns, repeat use. Now, your money anointing, coupled with your passion for youth, the elderly, the homeless or those in prison, is a recipe for success to be fruitful, multiply, replenish, subdue and dominate.

Once you determine your knowledge, skills and abilities, **write them down**. A lot of times people have thoughts and visions in their head. When they don't write them down, they can't begin to devise a plan of action. Instead, they walk around day dreaming and then they look up one day and see the very thing that God gave them to do done by someone else that devised a plan of action. So write the vision and make it plain.

Some of you may discover that you need to take a class or two in your area of expertise so that you can not only operate in your gift but become an expert at what you do so that you will **be the "go to" person**, the change agent or the trend setter to the glory of God. Once you become an expert in your field, you will then need to start seeing how your knowledge, skills and abilities play a role in doing what you are passionate about and created to do.

Here is how I see this played out based on my experience with the Lord: if you listed that you know how to cook, couple that with your passion and concern that you have for children eating healthy. Then spend time with the Lord in prayer so that he can **reveal to you your money anointing**. You then will be empowered by the Holy Ghost with your money anointing to have the answer to healthy eating based on the Word of God. The Book Of Leviticus in the Bible is a great resource for doing research on foods that are good for our health.

After you have spent time with God and studied the Word on healthy foods, you then will be empowered to design healthy recipes. Just as Moses was favored with Bezaleel, you too will begin to experience the favor of God and man.

Here are some things you can begin to see manifest:

1. You will be given favor to meet the right person in the school system to get your healthy recipes on the school's menu.

2. As others begin to hear about what you have been empowered to do, you will be asked to cook privately for those who need to get their body healthy.

3. This influence will also position you to be asked to speak publicly about cooking healthy.

4. Your healthy foods can then expand from the local schools to all the schools in the state.

5. As you are known as the expert, you will then teach others the system for coming up with healthy foods in order to reproduce after your own kind.

6. Because of the internet, you will be able to minister to the whole world from the comfort of your home about eating healthy via your website and internet marketing.

7. You then can leave a legacy by writing a book on healthy eating that will be a number one best seller and write a family recipe book on healthy eating that will be passed down to your children's children.

8. You can have a charitable foundation setup in honor of healthy eating to raise money for disadvantaged families who can't afford to eat healthy, or to raise money for a cure from the effects of not eating healthy such as diabetes, heart disease and cancer.

9. You can open up your own party land where kids can come have their party that has healthy fun foods to eat with games centered around healthy foods.

10. You can have thank you gifts that are focused on healthy foods, activity books on healthy eating, and even souvenir t-shirts with your slogan about eating healthy.

11. You can also start a school where healthy cooking is done for you to teach what you have learned to others so that they can get certification to do the same thing.

I can go on but I believe you get the point. Don't get worried about operating in your money anointing because of a bad economy. Just as the brook dried up for Elijah in **I Kings 17:7** because there was no rain, verse 8 says "and the word of the Lord came to him saying" – in other words, God provided another resource for him. This too will happen for you as you continue to spend time in prayer, walk in obedience and become more kingdom focused. Your new resource may be creating healthy food for pets, healthy food for those with diabetes, high blood pressure, etc.

I know you are saying wow, and I know that your creativity is beginning to wake up – **stir up your gift** that is what I have been empowered to do by the Holy Ghost. I am just like Mary when it comes to creativity. When she was pregnant with Jesus and went to tell Elizabeth that she was pregnant, Elizabeth baby leaped – so let your baby leap, birth it, get it out on the table, do the thing that you were put on this earth to do and let the Lord bring life to it.

Cast down those negative thoughts right now that are telling you that you can't do it. You can do all things through Christ who strengthens you. Don't be like the wicked servant in **Matthew 25:10** who was given one talent according to his knowledge, skills and abilities but did nothing with it. As you read on down to **Matthew 25:28** you will see that he was called wicked and his gift was taken from him and given to the one who was a good steward and already operating in his money anointing. I'm quite sure you don't want this to happen to you.

The reason I can talk about creativity with assurance is because this is how

God showed me my money anointing and what He does for one he will do for another, for **Romans 2:11** says "For there is no respect of person with God." This is what happened to me, as I spent time with God in prayer, God began to reveal to me creative ideas. This is how my kneeling prayer pillow, children's pillows, lap shawls, book publishing, The 90/10 Steward – I Love Therefore I Give Financial Fun Workshop and Track It Slips came to fruition.

Even when I was a teenage, I operated in my knowledge, skills and ability and tapped into my money anointing as I discovered that I was good at writing, typing and math. This coupled with the compassion I had for my mom who had 5 kids and worked several jobs to keep a roof over our head and feed us positioned me to be empowered by God to help out financially.

These are some of the things I did as I tapped into my money anointing as a teenager:

1. I typed papers for students who didn't want to type their papers for school.

2. I filled out income tax forms during tax season for other teens.

3. I tutored those who needed help in Algebra.

4. I had several babysitting jobs.

5. I worked in the cafeteria at a university since I loved to cook.

6. I sold icebergs (frozen Hawaiian punch with fruit cocktails).

7. I had house parties that I charged a fee to get in.

I was obedient in tithing so God blessed me accordingly. I had several streams of income as a teenager and now that I am an adult I still have several streams of income from my employment several businesses and investments. To God be the glory for all the wonderful things He has done. Now, I am here to help you. It is high time for you to wake out of sleep and begin to get busy for the kingdom. So set your mind to seek God's kingdom first. Your knowledge, skills and abilities coupled with your compassion for the things of God is a recipe for success to obtaining wealth. You too will be instrumental in financing the kingdom to reap the end time of harvest of souls.

CONCLUSION: Here is your plan of action:

First, find a time to sit down and evaluate your knowledge, skills and abilities.

Second, determine what you are passionate about based on Luke 4:18. This is what is going to happen: as you spend time with God in prayer with a heart wanting to do the will of God, He will reveal to you your assignment.

Third, make sure to have a pen and paper with you at all times so that you can write down every revelation. Your assignment is going to be based on the problem that you were put on this earth to solve – that is why you are so passionate about certain things. You will also see that you have already been operating in your gift.

Forth, based on the example I gave earlier about your money anointing being healthy foods, God will give you a company name, the design for a logo and a slogan. The name might be something like "I Can Make It Healthy". You will need to act fast and do the research to make sure that the name is not used already by someone else in business in your state. Once you check that out, pay to have a business license using that name.

Fifth, go on the internet to godaddy.com to buy the domain name "I Can Make It Healthy.com" to use on the internet for your website.

Sixth, create an email account using your business name at google. Hopefully your business name will be available so that your email name will be Icanmakeithealthy@gmail.com

Seventh, setup an online presence by creating a blog using blogger.com since it is free to use and easy to do. You will meet more prospects online than you could ever meet offline. Name your blog "I Can Make It Healthy".

Eighth, create a Facebook, Youtube and Twitter account with your business name "I Can Make It Healthy".

Ninth, create some business cards at Vistaprint.com with your business name, slogan and logo on it. They have specials and discounts regularly.

Tenth, go to your local Small Business Administration or Chamber Of Commerce so you can get all the other business needs such as help with a business plan and to network with other business owners.

ASSIGNMENT: Populate the **"My Knowledge, Skills & Abilities Worksheet"** with the revelation God has revealed to you during your time of prayer.

PRAYER: Dear Heavenly Father, I pray that this teaching would take root today in the hearts and minds of your people for **Revelations 2:29** says "He that have an ear, let him hear what the Spirit saith unto the church." Let us be doers of your word and not just hearers.

Help us to spend time with you in prayer so that you can reveal to us the skills, knowledge and abilities that we already have in order to tap into our money anointing. Empower us with your spirit to obtain the wealth so that we can be instrumental in financing the kingdom for the end time harvest of souls. In Jesus name Amen.

MY KNOWLEDGE SKILLS & ABILITIES WORKSHEET

NAME: _____

Exodus 31:3 "And I have filled him with the Spirit of God, with skill, ability and knowledge of all kinds of crafts." NIV

Knowledge:

_____

_____

_____

_____

Skills:

_____

_____

_____

_____

Abilities:

_____

_____

_____

_____

7 WHAT DO YOU THINK ABOUT YOUR TAX WITHHOLDINGS?

SCRIPTURE: **Matthew 22:15-21** *"Then went the Pharisees, and took counsel how they might entangle him in his talk. And they sent out unto him their disciples with the Herodians, saying, Master, we know that thou art true, and teachest the way of God in truth, neither carest thou for any man: for thou regardest not the person of men. Tell us therefore, What thinkest thou? Is it lawful to give tribute unto Caesar, or not? But Jesus perceived their wickedness, and said, Why tempt ye me, ye hypocrites? Shew me the tribute money. And they brought unto him a penny. And he saith unto them, Whose is this image and superscription? They say unto him, Caesar's. Then saith he unto them, Render therefore unto Caesar the things which are Caesar's; and unto God the things that are God's."*

TOPIC: What Do You Think About Your Tax Withholdings?

PRAYER: Dear Heavenly Father, thank you for your word for your word is true. Help us to apply your word to everything we do so that we can continue to bring glory and honor to your name. We will take advantage of opportunities, become forward thinkers and seek ways to maintain the wealth you have entrusted us with, in Jesus name we pray, Amen.

REVIEW: In the previous chapter, we discussed the second way to help with the debt elimination process and what it takes to obtain wealth in order to generate extra money. In that teaching, I showed you how you could utilize your knowledge, skills and abilities to generate extra income. Also, I showed you how you could use the thing that you love to do and may already be doing to start earning income from offering it as a product or service.

For those of you who did not know what your **knowledge, skills and abilities** were, I pray that you spent time with God in prayer to get revelation. Revelation so you can begin to operate in the thing that you were put on this earth to do. You then can be a blessing to yourself, as well as the kingdom of God and position yourself to leave an inheritance for your children's children.

For those of you who participated in the last chapter's exercise and have decided that you want to earn an income online from the thing that God revealed to you, I can provide you with the tools to show you how to get everything setup to have an online presence and earn extra income.

I will show you how to earn money online with as little as zero to $100 investment. This is what God revealed to me as I spent time with Him for revelation of how to earn extra income based on my knowledge, skills and abilities. God is no respecter of person, so just like he gave me this revelation, he will do the same thing for you. Let's thank God for the wonderful relationship that we have with Him as our Heavenly Father. If you are interested in pursuing this opportunity, send me an email at tjandtjenterprise@gmail.com

When we reviewed the Creditor Debt Elimination Worksheet, we discussed the **first** concept to start your debt elimination process. You were to determine where you can cutback to have an extra $25, $50 or whatever amount you determined you needed to start paying off your first creditor until all debt is eliminated.

In this chapter, we will discuss in details the **third** way to assist in the debt elimination process by using your tax withholdings.

THE THIRD DEBT ELIMINATION IDEA

TAX WITHHOLDINGS: In this chapter, we will talk about the **third** way we can get started with our debt elimination process and maintain our wealth. We will pursue this by taking advantage of our tax withholdings refund from our favorite place – The Internal Revenue Service or The IRS affectionately known as Uncle Sam.

Every year during tax season, you should consider using your tax withholdings refund as a great way to get a jump start in your debt elimination process to maintain wealth.

Let's look at the definition of **tax withholdings** according to Merriam Webster – it is "a deduction from wages, fees or dividends levied at a source of income as advance payment on income tax."

As we look at our scripture for today, Matthew 22:17-21 we see where the Pharisees tried to trip up Jesus by asking him about whether taxes should be paid.

Let's read those same scriptures in the NIV version which says *"Then the Pharisees went out and laid plans to trap him in his words. They sent their disciples to him along with the Herodians. "Teacher," they said, "we know you are a man of integrity and that you teach the way of God in accordance with the truth. You aren't swayed by men, because you pay no attention to who they are. Tell us then, what is your opinion? Is it right to pay taxes to Caesar or not?"*

But Jesus, knowing their evil intent, said, you hypocrites, why are you trying to trap me? Show me the coin used for paying the tax. They brought him a denarius, and he asked them, "Whose portrait is this? And whose inscription?" Caesar's, they replied. Then he said to them, "Give to Caesar what is Caesar's, and to God what is God's."

Now why or how did the Pharisees think that they could trap the all knowing, the all wise, omnipotent Jesus, go figure. The point I want to elaborate on is that Jesus said to give to Caesar what is Caesar and to God what is God's. In saying that, he is saying that they are to honor the law of the land which was established by Caesar in **Luke 2:1** which says *"And it came to pass in those days that there went out a decree from Caesar Augustus that all the world should be taxed"*.

In reference to the second statement by Jesus, "give to God what is God's," he wanted them to know that honor is to be given to God's law also. This law was established in **Leviticus 27:30** which says *"And all the tithe of the land, whether of the seed of the land, or of the fruit of the tree is the Lord's, it is Holy unto the Lord."*

So these two concepts of rendering to Caesar and to God are to be obeyed by us in the 21st century even though they were established a long time ago. Now we don't have a choice about paying Uncle Sam his taxes because everything is in place for that to automatically happen. But for some reason, since there isn't anything put in place to automatically draft our tithes from our wages, some feel that they have a choice about paying tithes.

When you **pay taxes**, you are demonstrating the following acts to our governmental system:

Honor - You are demonstrating honor to the civil government where you live as it provides protection
Obedience - You are demonstrating obedience as you obey the laws that are in place to suppress evil doings
Tribute - You are demonstrating tribute as you contribute to the expenses incurred by the government

When you **pay tithes**, you are demonstrating the following acts to our

Lord and Saviour:

Honor – You are acknowledging God as the creator of all things and your source

Obedience – You are complying to God's commands so that his kingdom can be established here on earth

Tribute – You are offering thanks to God as you give in faith according to his promises

Here are the **benefits** of offering honor, obedience and tribute to the IRS when you pay your taxes:

- ✓ You keep yourself out of harm's way by not going to jail if you don't pay your taxes – We all have seen time after time, big name celebrities go to jail for refusing to pay income taxes
- ✓ You are helping to stimulate the economy –the majority of the people who get income tax refund checks go out and buy the things that they have been dying to get such as big screen tvs, cars, electronic items, clothes, just to name a few , and
- ✓ You are creating a way for you to have a lump sum payment once a year to take advantage of – this is the ideal thing to do with your tax refund but I don't have stats of how many people actually do this.

Of course all of these things are possible if you figured out your tax return properly; otherwise, you may have to add to the tax withholding already taken out of your pay during the year. Therefore, at the end of the tax season, instead of getting a tax refund, you have to write a check to the IRS.

Here are the **benefits** of offering honor, obedience and tribute to God by paying the tithes:

- You are giving God the opportunity to prove Himself to be a blessing to you according to **Malachi 3:10** which says *"Bring me all the tithes into the storehouse that there may be meat in mine house and prove me now herewith saith the Lord of hosts if I will not open you the windows of heaven and pour you out a blessing that there shall not be room enough to receive it."*
- You are protecting your blessing from the enemy according to

Malachi 3:11 which says *"And I will rebuke the devourer for your sakes and he shall not destroy the fruits of your ground, neither shall your vine cast her fruit before the time in the field saith the Lord of hosts."*

- You are pleasing to God and an example to others of being a good steward according to **Malachi 3:12** which says *"And all nations shall call you blessed for you shall be a delightsome land saith the Lord of hosts."*

Now let's take a look at this whole tax return concept and see if we are getting the most benefit from it. Now I'm going to believe that you are adhering to the wisdom given in one of the previous teachings pertaining to depreciating assets. Therefore, you know you should not be spending your return on depreciating or consumable assets. This asset is something you buy that if you tried to sell it a year later, you would not get a profit from it such as buying a new car, clothes, food, vacations, etc.

TAX REFUND USE

If you get a tax refund, here are some things you can use it for:

1 - Help accelerate your goal of becoming debt free.

2 - Invest it into a high interest bearing saving account, money market account or mutual funds.

3 – Upgrade your appliances to energy efficient appliances to help cut down on your electric bill.

4 –Start the business you want to pursue based on your knowledge, skills and abilities.

5 – Pay for a course that can make you promotable in the job that you are in or start a career that is in high demand.

6 – Be a blessing to someone you know that is unemployed or on a fixed income.

7 – Start a college fund.

8 – Add to your emergency fund account.

9 – Purchase an annuity or universal life policy with cash value.

10 – Purchase property.

I'm quite sure you can come up with a few more of your own. My husband and I can help you get started using your tax withholdings with any of the

10 concepts mentioned. If you need assistance, feel free to email us at tjandtjenterprise@gmail.com.

FUN ACCOUNT

Remember, our primary goal of our tax refund is to assist in becoming debt free. After you have determined the amount of your tax withholdings to use to help jump start your debt elimination process, you can now begin to invest a percentage of it to your fun account. Depending on the amount of your tax refund, you can put an additional 5% of it in your fun money account to cover your holiday happiness yearly expenses. I will review the different expenses to allocate funds for to populate this worksheet.

HOLIDAY HAPPINESS: Holiday Happiness is the worksheet that I devised to help you pre-plan the amount of money to spend based on the various holidays, birthdays or special occasions that occur throughout the year.

Keep in mind that 90/10 stewards are forward thinkers and always looking for ways to position themselves to be blessed as they contemplate their next financial move. **Habakkuk 2:2** says *"write the vision and make it plain upon tables that he may run that readeth it."*

Print a copy of the **Holiday Happiness Worksheet**. I will give you a few of the things that you may want to write down and then you can come up with the rest of them.

JANUARY: For the month of January, New Year's Day is celebrated. As an annual event, some families invite all of the family members over for a family breakfast or you may go out as a family to eat. Depending on how big your family is, this could be very costly so write down an amount for this event if this is something that is done in your family.

FEBRUARY: For the month of February, Valentine's Day is celebrated. In my house, this is a memorable time since my birthday is on Valentine's Day. For others, you may only have Valentine's Day to celebrate. So if you plan on buying flowers, candy, stuffed animals or going out to dinner, write down an amount for this event.

MARCH: For the month of March, St. Patrick's Day is celebrated. I don't believe a whole lot of money is spent on it but then sometimes Easter is in March so you may incur some expenses with it by purchasing things for your children or grandchildren. So come up with an amount to write down for this event if this is something you plan to celebrate.

APRIL: For the month of April, Easter may be in this month if it isn't in March. If not, this is the month that most people with homes may start working on beautifying their yard by buying new sod, flowers, mulch, etc. Even though this isn't a holiday, it definitely is an event that you want to plan for. So write down an amount for it.

MAY: For the month of May, Memorial Day is celebrated mostly with a family cookout. This could be costly so write down an amount to spend for this event.

JUNE: For the month of June, there isn't a holiday to celebrate but a lot of kids graduate from kindergartner, middle school, high school and college. This is also when the kids are out of school for the summer. You may want to write down an amount to spend on graduation gifts and trips the kids will be going on with their summer camps or visiting other relatives.

JULY: For the month of July, Fourth of July is celebrated. If you plan on cooking out and inviting others over, write down an amount to spend for this event.

AUGUST: For the month of August, there isn't a holiday to celebrate but the kids go back to school or start college education. Write down an amount that you may need to spend on activities surrounding the kids going back to school and college.

SEPTEMBER: For the month of September, Labor Day is celebrated. This is another day to cookout. Write down an amount you may spend for this holiday.

OCTOBER: For the month of October, most people start early Christmas shopping. So if you are an early shopper, write down an amount for this event.

NOVEMBER: For the month of November, Thanksgiving is celebrated. If you are cooking or even going to travel to visit relatives for this holiday, write down an amount for this event.

DECEMBER: For the month of December, Christmas and New Year's Eve are celebrated. If you are cooking, traveling and/or buying gifts for Christmas, come up with an amount for these activities as well as any celebrating you may be doing in honor of New Year's Eve.

CONCLUSION: I hope that you see that your tax withholdings refund can be a way for you to accelerate your goal of becoming debt free and have some fun throughout the year too. You can start building your wealth, be a blessing to the kingdom and become an end time financier. Now if this was not your thoughts about your tax withholdings, I want you to do what it says in **2 Corinthians 10:5** which reads *"casting down imaginations and every high thing that exalted itself against the knowledge of God and bringing into captivity every thought to the obedience of Christ."*

So the next time you get a tax refund, you will see it as a way to empower yourself financially. I want you to know that the Lord has already revealed to me and my husband that He is using us as end time financiers for His kingdom. And for those of you who have been participating in this train, you will also get the revelation that you are to play a role as an end time financier as well.

FINANCIER: A **financier** according to Merriam Webster Dictionary is **"one who deals with finance and investments on a large scale."** As you have heard me say on numerous occasions this is not about you, it is about your love of God and your assignment which is to advance the kingdom of God.

So this training is to position you to be an end time financier as a 90/10 steward in order for God's kingdom to be established on earth as we dominate the economy with our wealth.

ECONOMY: The definition of economy is **"a system of production**

and distribution and consumption or the efficient use of resources." As you look back at your Monthly Cashflow Statement, you will see how utilizing this is positioning you to affect change in your personal economy. For those of you who have been participating in this teaching and have not created your Monthly Cashflow Statement, go back through each chapter teaching and get caught up.

What we are teaching here are simple, practical and easy to implement concepts that will catapult you into your purpose and destiny. It is time out for getting excited about what God is going to do; instead, it is time to execute God's plan of action.

ASSIGNMENT: Populate your **Holiday Happiness Worksheet**. I pray that this teaching would take root today in the your heart and mind. For **James 2:24** says *"For as the body without the spirit is dead, so faith without works is dead also."* I believe that you are ready to be a doer of God's Word and not just a hearer.

Find a moment to spend time in prayer so that God can show you how to best use the refund checks you will receive in order to expedite your Debt Elimination process. Yearly print a Holiday Happiness Worksheet to pre-plan your expenses as you strive to manage the wealth you have been blessed to steward.

Lastly, thank God in advance for choosing you to be an end time financier. It is truly an honor to establish His kingdom here on earth to reap the end time harvest of souls.

HOLIDAY HAPPINESS

MONTH	EVENTS	PLANNED AMOUNT
JANUARY	_____	_____
	_____	_____
FEBRUARY	_____	_____
	_____	_____
MARCH	_____	_____
	_____	_____
APRIL	_____	_____
	_____	_____
MAY	_____	_____
	_____	_____
JUNE	_____	_____
	_____	_____
JULY	_____	_____
	_____	_____
AUGUST	_____	_____
	_____	_____
SEPTEMBER	_____	_____
	_____	_____
OCTOBER	_____	_____
	_____	_____
NOVEMBER	_____	_____
	_____	_____
DECEMBER	_____	_____

8 SEE WHAT GOD SAYS AND ACT ACCORDINGLY

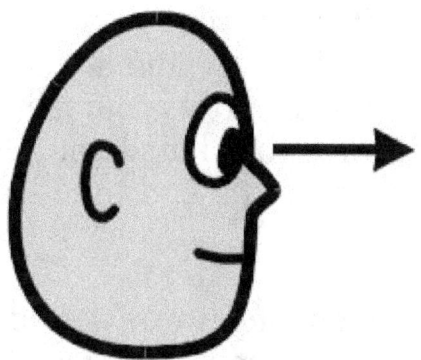

SCRIPTURE: **Numbers 13:17-20** *"And Moses sent them to spy out the land of Canaan, and said unto them, Get you up this way southward, and go up into the mountain and see the land, what it is; and the people that dwelleth therein, whether they be strong or weak, few or many; and what the land is that they dwell in, whether it be good or bad; and what cities they be that they dwell in, whether in tents, or in strong holds; and what the land is, whether it be fat or lean, whether there be wood therein, or not. And be ye of good courage, and bring of the fruit of the land. Now the time was the time of the first ripe grapes."*

Numbers 13:25-27 *"And they returned from searching of the land after forty days. And they went and came to Moses, and to Aaron, and to all* *the congregation of the children of Israel, unto the wilderness of Paran, to Kadesh; and brought back word unto them, and unto all the congregation, and shewed them the fruit of the land. And they told him, and said, We came unto the land whither thou sentest us, and surely it floweth with milk and honey; and this is the fruit of it."*

Numbers 13:30 *"And Caleb stilled the people before Moses, and said, Let us go up at once, and possess it; for we are well able to overcome it."*

TOPIC: See What God Says And Act Accordingly

PRAYER: Dear Heavenly Father, thank you for good leaders. Thank you for your word; help us to hide it in our hearts so that we won't sin against you. I pray that as we meditate on your word daily, it will empower us to step out in faith and see what you say and act accordingly. Help us to do the things that will be a blessing to us, our children and our children's children so that we can advance your kingdom. Thank you for choosing us to be end time financiers to reap the end time harvest of souls. In Jesus name Amen.

REVIEW: In the previous chapter we reviewed the third way to obtain wealth in order to generate extra money to assist in the debt elimination process and management of your wealth by taking advantage of our tax withholdings refund check from the IRS. I pray that you utilized this money to get a jump on starting your debt elimination process and manage your wealth.

We also discussed 10 ways that you could get the most benefit out of your tax withholdings and the components of the worksheet **Holiday Happiness**. This worksheet can be used to pre-plan the amount of money you will spend based on the various holidays, birthdays or special occasions that occur throughout the year. Also, this worksheet was developed because 90/10 stewards are forward thinkers and always looking for ways to position themselves to be blessed and a blessing as they contemplate their next financial move.

SEE WHAT GOD SAYS: In this chapter, we will talk about how to "See what God says and Act Accordingly" based on our topic for today. So let's get started.

As we look at our scripture for today, we see that Moses sent out spies to spy out the promised land. He sent 12 spies, one from each of the tribes according to Numbers 13:3 which says *"And Moses by the commandment of the Lord sent them from the wilderness of Paran: all those men were heads of the children of Israel."* So since these were heads of the tribe, it means that these were the leaders.

LEADER: Let's look at the definition of a leader according to Merriam Webster dictionary – a leader is **"one who leads, a person that leads, a person that directs, the first or principle office of a group and one who ranks first."** Based on past experiences, if I'm going to pick someone to do a job for me, I'm going to choose someone that I believe is capable of carrying out my commands or orders as a leader.

This concept of having a leader takes place in all kinds of settings such as on our jobs when there are meetings, projects and events. The leader in our family is the person coordinating the meetings for family reunions, funerals, etc. This person makes sure all arrangements take place and are setup. In group settings such as girl or boy scout troops, sororities and fraternities, there's always a leader. In the church, there are leaders for various programs and ministries, etc. such as evangelism, jails/prison and food/clothing ministry.

So basically, there is always someone leading – whether appointed or they just choose to step up to the plate on their own once they see no one leading.

I have experienced some good leaders and then I have experienced some bad leaders and when I see there is a bad leader, immediately I kick into "I'm going to be the leader" mode. I don't know how many of you are like this but I refuse to follow someone who isn't capable of leading. People look up to leaders because of their expertise. Leaders are also people of influence – good or bad. Since the highly respected leaders of the tribes were sent to spy out the land, this means the tribes were going to hang on every word they said.

SCOUT OUT THE LAND: Now let's look at what happened when these 12 leaders went to spy out the land. Out of the 12 that went to spy out the land, only 2 of them came back and reported to the people a good report because they saw what God said and wanted to act accordingly.

This is what happened when they came back after 40 days of scouting out the land based on **Nehemiah 13:26-31** in the NIV Bible which reads "They came back to Moses and Aaron and the whole Israelite community at Kadesh in the Desert of Paran. There they reported to them and to the whole assembly and showed them the fruit of the land. They gave Moses this account: "We went into the land to which you sent us, and it does flow with milk and honey! Here is its fruit.

Now if it was me, they wouldn't have to say another word – I would have started dancing like David danced and shouted like the children of Israel did when the walls of Jericho fell down. When you heard in the previous chapter that you have been chosen to be an end time financier for the kingdom of God, you should have had your baby leap inside of you and got encouraged knowing that out of all the people in the world, the Lord has chosen you for such a time as this to possess the land.

SEE WHAT GOD SAYS CASE STUDY

I can give you proof of this since my husband and I have been chosen to be end time financiers ourselves. We heard a Word from God about possessing some land so that we can leave an inheritance to our children and we believed God. My husband started looking at purchasing tax deed property in Georgia. He was told that this would be hard to do since only certain people know how to do it and won't let others in on how it is done (you know the good old boys system). We did not let that bother us.

Here is what we did in faith:

1. We registered a business name to purchase the property in so there could be no discrimination
2. Opened up a business account
3. Placed the small amount of money we had in it
4. Prayed at the steps of the court building where the tax deed sales take

place Researched the properties we wanted to purchase
5. Went to the tax deed sale
6. Walked away with 3 properties!

Now I would have to say that this is a good report.

There are people who live in Georgia that want to do this and can't. We don't even reside there and got passed all the barriers and systems in place that were hard to get through because of the favor of the Lord. The money generated from these properties will definitely be used to help us build our wealth and be a blessing in the kingdom of God. I thank the Lord for having a husband who is a good leader as the head of our home and can see what God says in his Word and act accordingly.

This is what we want to happen in your homes and I'm going to believe that this will happen in the name of Jesus – Amen. Putting this training together was a challenge and I could have decided that I could not do it since I work a full time job. But because I stepped out on faith, God gave me the creativity I needed so I could be in two places at the same time – on my job and producing this training through the use of technology - Halleluah.

Now in our scripture for today, instead of all 12 leaders leaving the people with a good report so they could "see what God says and act accordingly, this is what they also said in **Numbers 13:28-30** "But the people who live there are powerful, and the cities are fortified and very large. We even saw descendants of Anak there. The Amalekites live in the Negev; the Hittites, Jebusites and Amorites live in the hill country; and the Canaanites live near the sea and along the Jordan.

CALEB: Then Caleb silenced the people before Moses and said, we should go up and take possession of the land, for we can certainly do it." Now thank God for leaders who do "see what God says and act accordingly". Caleb is an example of a good leader.

In other words, Caleb is letting them know that they are giving out too much information to the point that what sounded good at first is now starting to not look so good after all. It would not have been a problem with them giving them all the details because Moses did ask them to come back with this information so the people could know what they were facing.

A perfect example of this same kind of scenario would be, creating your **Cashflow Statement** and your **Debt Elimination Worksheet** and praying to God to show you how to implement discipline to become debt free and obtain wealth. Then once he shows you what to do, you then decide that it isn't possible because of what you see on your worksheet or what you see on tv or what you see going on with other's financial situation.

Or here's another scenario, your leader in the ministry hears a Word from God that says the church is going to go out two by two, door to door in a certain neighborhood and bless each household with bags of goodies. Instead of you trusting God, you decide that you need a bag of goodies yourself and question why you should participate in the outreach. Well the reason you want to participate is because if God says it, then that settles it, plain and simple -God wants us to trust him, believe him and operate in faith.

Here's where the Israelites went wrong based on **Nehemiah 13:31-33** which reads "But the men who had gone up with him (Caleb) said, we can't attack those people; they are stronger than we are. And they spread among the Israelites a bad report about the land they had explored. They said, "The land we explored devours those living in it. All the people we saw there are of great size. We saw the Nephilim there (the descendants of Anak come from the Nephilim). We seemed like grasshoppers in our own eyes, and we looked the same to them."

Now tell me how can they talk foolishly like this when they spent 40 days over there scouting out the land and came back with proof that the land really does flow with milk and honey? When I read the last part of this passage, I was disappointed and just like I was disappointed, God was disappointed as well but we'll talk about that in a minute.

JOSHUA: Now let me show you the other leader who gave a good report which was Joshua in **Numbers 14:6-9** which reads "Joshua son of Nun and Caleb son of Jephunneh, who were among those who had explored the land, tore their clothes and said to the entire Israelite assembly, "The land we passed through and explored is exceedingly good. If the LORD is pleased with us, he will lead us into that land, a land flowing with milk and honey, and will give it to us. Only do not rebel against the LORD. And do not be afraid of the people of the land, because we will swallow them up. **Their protection is gone**, but the LORD is with us. Do not be afraid of them." This kind of talk pleased God and this is what he is looking for you to do as you execute discipline in your finances.

COMPLAINTS: Know that when God says to do something, he wants you to do it in expectation of knowing that His Word is good and that He is who He says He is – your provider, your protector, your rewarder and so on and so forth. But let's look at what God's response was to this rebellion that took place by the 10 leaders according to **Numbers 14:26-35** which reads "The LORD said to Moses and Aaron: "How long will this wicked community grumble against me? I have heard the complaints of these grumbling Israelites.

So tell them, 'As surely as I live, declares the LORD, I will do to you the very things I heard you say: In this desert your bodies will fall — every one of you twenty years old or more who was counted in the census and who has grumbled against me. Not one of you will enter the land I swore with uplifted hand to make your home, except Caleb son of Jephunneh and Joshua son of Nun.

As for your children that you said would be taken as plunder, I will bring them in to enjoy the land you have rejected. But you — your bodies will fall in this desert. Your children will be shepherds here for forty years, suffering for your unfaithfulness, until the last of your bodies lies in the desert. For forty years — one year for each of the forty days you explored the land — you will suffer for your sins and know what it is like to have me against you.' I, the LORD, have spoken, and I will surely do these things to this whole wicked community, which has banded together against me. They will meet their end in this desert; here they will die."

This says to me that God really wants us to obtain all the blessings he has already said we can have. But if you don't believe that he wants you to prosper, if you don't believe that you are to possess lands and houses, if you don't believe that you are to be wealthy then guess what, you won't. Not only will you have happen to you what you believe, your children will also suffer because of your unbelief and unfaithfulness. As new testament believers, Jesus wants us to have faith in God according to **Mark 11:22 NIV**.

Now I pose a question to you. **Are you a leader in your home?** Are you seeing what God says and acting accordingly? If you aren't, I'm here on assignment as God's chosen leader in the area of finances to move you from exalting what you see and hear in the natural over God's word which is supernatural. God's word is spirit and gives life to any situation that seems to be dead. His word is true for He said "I am the way, the truth and the life" – His word is sharp and powerful enough for you to speak a word over your financial situation and have it to come to pass – though it tarry wait on it, for it will speak and not lie.

By the power of the Almighty God, you have been empowered to cast down imaginations and thoughts that try to exalt itself against the knowledge of God. As mentioned earlier, my husband and I have been placed in the kingdom for such a time as this to equip the body with the tools necessary to possess the land that flows with milk and honey and become end time financiers for the kingdom of God.

Jesus is soon to return and he needs people of faith on point and strategically placed throughout the kingdom to do his good and perfect will. It is great, awesome and wonderful that you are saved, attend church regularly and even working in ministry but this assignment is bigger than you and me.

Jesus said in **John 14:12-15** *"Verily, verily, I say unto you, He that believeth on me, the works that I do shall he do also; and greater works than these shall he do; because I go unto my Father. And whatsoever ye shall ask in my name, that will I do, that the Father may be glorified in the Son. If ye shall ask any thing in my name, I will do it. If ye love me, keep my commandments."* This whole money thing or wealth thing or economy thing is about love.

There are numerous scriptures commanding us to keep God's commandment to love one another, love the children of God, love our neighbors, the poor, the widows, the orphans, etc. So when we show love towards one another, it is as if we are showing love towards God himself and we get to experience God right here on earth because **I John 4:16** says that God is love.

If you have not been trusting and believing God's word and walking in faith, you need to repent and ask the Lord to open your eyes so that you can see what he says and act according in love, trust and faith, not fear, doubt or unbelief.

Now let's talk about what it takes to be a good leader in your home with your finances.

First, make a declaration that you are going to implement the disciplines necessary to become a 90/10 steward which means you are going to tithe 10% and implement financial discipline with the other 90% according to the 90/10 steward concept.

Second, create your Monthly Cashflow Statement, your Debt Elimination Worksheet and do all the other assignments that I have given you in these trainings as 90/10 stewards.

Third, sit down with your family and let everybody in on this so that you can pass down financial discipline to your children and your children's children. For **Deuteronomy 11:26** says *"I set before you this day a blessing and a curse; a blessing if you obey his commands or a curse if you don't obey his commands."* This is a serious matter. I don't know about you, but I want to obey God and receive all of his blessings. Not only for me, but I want my friends blessed, my neighbors blessed, my family blessed and my brothers and sisters in Christ blessed.

Let's talk about why you should teach your children to be 90/10 stewards. **Genesis 1:28** *says "And God blessed them, and God said unto them, Be fruitful , and multiply, and replenish the earth, and subdue it: and have dominion over the fish of the sea, and over the fowl of the air, and over every living thing that moveth upon the earth."*

So what that says is, we will produce fruit whether it is good fruit or bad. As a good leader, we want to produce good fruit so that our children can taste and see that the Lord is good. You want your children to love the Lord and be another you wherever they go and with whatever they pursue in life. This is so that the earth can be replenished with more of the love of God.

We should be the standard, the ones respected and revered so that we can subdue and have dominion in whatever arena we enter whether that is the school system, the judicial system, corporate America, etc. You've seen it before, the great grandfather was a doctor or a lawyer, the grandfather is a doctor or lawyer, the father is a doctor or lawyer and the young son is pretending to be a doctor or lawyer.

It's no different in the supernatural, the great grandfather was a known evangelist or teacher, the grandfather was a known evangelist or teacher, the father is known for his evangelist ministering or teaching and the child is evangelizing everybody in their neighborhood or classroom. I have people tell me all the time that my daughter is just like me.

TITHING CASE STUDY

CASE STUDY: My daughter started tithing at 7 years old from the money she would get as gifts from her birthday parties and not only did she tithe 10% but she also gave to our pastor personally. And even at a young age, I'm not sure if she was 8 or 9 but I remember when one of her friends came over after having her birthday party and told my daughter that she got a total of $40 for her birthday. So my daughter told her "now you know you need to tithe 10% of it." Her friend said ok. How much would that be? My daughter said $4. The little girl said $4 is a lot of money, I'll tithe $2. Well, at least she gave something. You get my point here.

It is so much easier teaching kids when they are young because they want to be like mom or dad so they put on your shoes, shirts and hats trying to look like you so why not teach them to look like you financially. The one thing about kids is that they do what you do and not what you say so keep that in mind.

Our goal should be to teach our kids to be responsible enough so that when they go off to college, they won't get into a whole lot of debt before they can get their degree and end up going into marriage already in financial ruin.

Statistics shows that the number one reason for divorce is money. So let's strive to teach our children to tithe 10%, and implement discipline with the other 90% so that they will also become 90/10 stewards.

CONCLUSION: You have been equipped with the disciplines in this training to become debt free, a lender not a borrower, and a giver of a dime out of a dollar. You know how not to be fearful like the 10 leaders who rebelled against God by not believing that He was going to do what He said He would do. You know how to see your bills and say, I can tithe and pay my bills.

You will possess the land, you will leave an inheritance to your children's children, you will be a change agent in the kingdom of God, you will be a person of influence and considered a leader in every arena you enter.

You will tap into your God given creativity so that your dreams will come forth, your visions will come forth, your aspirations will come forth even if they have laid dormant to the point that it stinketh like Lazarus did. I am here to let you know that there is resurrection power in the blood of Jesus Christ. So rise up, see what God says and act accordingly!

ASSIGNMENT: Your assignment is to populate the **I See It, Say It, and Do It** worksheet with words to empower you to see what God says and act accordingly. Here's an example:

I see myself blessed according to Deuteronomy 28:8
I see myself being a blessing to the kingdom – Genesis 22:17-18
I see myself debt free – II Kings 4:17
I see myself as an end time financier – Matthew 25:35-36
I see myself living a long healthy and prosperous life – 3 John 2:2
I see myself wealthy – Deuteronomy 8:18
I see myself leaving a legacy behind – Proverbs 13:22
I see myself highly favored – Proverbs 3:4
I see myself living a peaceful life – Isaiah 26:3
I see myself being a lender and not a borrower – Deuteronomy 15:6
I see myself making right choices and decisions – Proverbs 16:9

You can use these or come up with your own. The intent is for you to get the word of God in you so that you can increase your faith and believe God.

I decree and declare this for you today as you eat, sleep and drink the Word of God, morning night and noon:

- You will increase your faith and do those things that are pleasing to the Lord.

- You will be like a tree planted by rivers of living water and bring forth your fruit in its season.

- You are going to take what you hear from these teachings and glean off of them to propel your dreams, talents and gifts into flight.

I SEE IT, SAY IT AND DO IT!

I see myself _____

I see myself _____

I see myself _____

I see myself _____

I see myself _____

I see myself _____

I see myself _____

I see myself _____

I see myself _____

I see myself _____

I see myself _____

I see myself _____

I see myself _____

I see myself _____

I see myself _____

I see myself _____

9 LET'S CONSIDER THE ANT A STRATEGIST

SCRIPTURE: Proverbs 6:6-8 *"Go to the ant thou sluggard; consider her ways and be wise: which having no guide, overseer, or ruler, provideth her meat in the summer and gathereth her food in the harvest."*

TOPIC: Let's Consider The Ant A Strategist

PRAYER: Dear Heavenly Father, thank you for creating the ant. Help us consider the ant when we begin to see ourselves slipping, becoming sluggish, lethargic or lazy. Anoint our mind and give us an ear to hear what you are saying as we consider the ant according to your Word.

REVIEW: In the previous chapter we gave strategies on how to see what God says and act accordingly. In that teaching, we looked at the 90/10 steward as a leader. As an assignment, you were to populate a worksheet "**I See It, Say It And Do It**" that have words to empower you to see what God says and act accordingly. For those of you who created this worksheet, you should have a testimony of how your faith has been taken to another level and you should be operating in another realm supernaturally. Let's move on to this chapter's topic.

A STRATEGIST: In this chapter, we will talk about the ant based on our topic for today "Let's consider the ant a strategist". The definition of a strategist according to Merriam Webster dictionary **is "a person skilled in strategy."** Now the definition of **strategy** is **"a careful plan or method, the art of devising or employing plans towards a goal."** As we go through this teaching, you will see that the ant is a strategist and that it definitely is not a sluggard.

SLUGGARD: As we look at our scripture for today, we see that a sluggard is to go to the ant to consider her ways and be wise. Let's look at the definition of a sluggard according to Merriam Webster dictionary. **A sluggard is "a habitually lazy person."**

Now you may be wondering what does being lazy have to do with being a 90/10 steward. I'm glad you are curious. I'm going to believe that you are not a sluggard but if you are, I am here to help you implement kingdom strategies to counteract this spirit so that you can operate in wisdom and become a strategist.

Based on our teaching from **Proverbs 6:6** "go to the ant thou sluggard consider her ways and be wise", if you are a sluggard or lazy, you will not implement the discipline it takes to become a 90/10 steward. Also, you will not implement wisdom if you are too lazy to do what it takes to get the wisdom. There is good news! We are here to help you implement kingdom strategies to counteract laziness so you can move forward with wisdom and become a strategist.

Let's look at the consequences of being a sluggard or lazy according to the Word.

- **Proverbs 13:4** The sluggard craves and gets nothing, but the desires of the diligent are fully satisfied.
- **Proberbs 15:19** The way of the sluggard is blocked with thorns, but the path of the upright is a highway.
- **Proverbs 20:4** A sluggard does not plow in season so at harvest time he looks and finds nothing.
- **Proverbs 21:25** The sluggards craving will be the death of him because his hand refuse to work.
- **Hebrews 6:12** That ye be not slothful, but followers of them who through faith and patience inherit the promises. We do not want you to become lazy, but imitate those who through faith and patience inherit what has been promised.

Remember in the previous chapter, we talked about seeing what God says and acting accordingly. We talked about seeing ourselves wealthy, leaving an inheritance, so on and so forth. If you are lazy none of these things will happen.

ANTS: I also went to the Encyclopedia to find out more about ants since the scripture says to consider the ant and in order for me to consider the ant, I had to do some research. Here is what I found:

1. Ants are social, and nest in tunnels or galleries in the soil under a dome or hill of sand or debris.

2. There are mound building ants who construct the hill. The ants you see are the workers. Ants of the worker type may become soldiers or members of other specialized castes.

3. Some of the ants are called "harvester ants" because they eat and store seeds. They travel like armies in long columns overrunning and devouring animals that cannot flee their path.

4. The African ants even consume large mammals.

CAUSES OF LAZINESS

Let's explore laziness. There are several factors that contribute to laziness and a lack of action. I will discuss in details some of them and the strategies to implement to conquer them.

1. **First Cause - Not taking notice of yourself**

Pay attention to your mood, temperance and attitude. Just like there are 4 seasons, summer, winter, spring and fall, your mood, temperance and attitude is different during those seasons.

For example, in the summer time, people get lazy because it is so hot. If you notice this about yourself, come up with a strategy to counteract this reason for being lazy with something that will empower you.

In other words, be strategic like the ant and get up early in the morning, write down goals and get as much done before the temperature gets too hot. As I mentioned early, the summer is when the ants reap their harvest. They store up seed for the winter. So, do what **Romans 12:11** says which is to "never be lacking in zeal but keep your spiritual fervor, serving the Lord."

In order to move out of laziness in this instance, you are going to have to become like the harvester ant. Take notice of yourself and determine your gift. We talked about this in one of the previous teachings so I won't go into depth on that. For instance, if you have a business that is seasonal such as a car wash or window tinting service and the summer is when you get the most business, then the summer is harvest time for you.

Make sure to do everything with the power that was given to you by the Holy Ghost and be like the harvester ant and take advantage of this season to reap your harvest. For **Genesis 8:22** says "while the earth remaineth, seedtime and harvest, and cold and heat and summer and winter, and day and night shall not cease." So determine what season you are in and start planning how to continue to be in seedtime so that you will have a perpetual harvest.

STRATEGY: As the owner of a car wash or window tinting service, yes your greatest harvest will be in the **summer** but there are 3 other seasons that you can take advantage of when you take notice of yourself and your gift. For example, if you feel more laid back or reserved during the **winter** season since it is cold, maybe this could be the time for you to do email marketing to attract new clients.

If you realize that you like playing a role in the acquisition of new things that come out which is in the **spring**, maybe you could approach car dealerships when the new cars come out to get a contract to tint the windows of the new cars.

In the **fall**, if you rather be inside more than outside, you can solicit condo or home owners to tint their residence to acquire contracts during that season. Now if you are lazy and don't know your purpose or gift, you won't be able to do these things. I'm quite sure you get the picture here – so consider the harvester ant the strategist and devise a plan.

2. Second Cause - You tried something and it didn't work

The reason laziness creeps in with this cause is due to a lack of due diligence, not counting up the cost, trying to be like the Jones', getting in over your head and moving too quick because of being anxious.

For instance, you decided to buy a house. After you get the house, you realize that you were going to need a lawn mower to cut the grass, an edger, a weed eater, etc. Now you are disgusted because you don't have the funds so you start to slip into lazy mode. The way you are to counteract this type of laziness is by doing what **Luke 14:28** says "suppose one of you wants to build a tower. Will he not first sit down and estimate the cost to see if he has enough money to complete it?"

STRATEGY: Take notice and be like the mound building ants if this form of laziness creeps up. Determine all the cost involved upfront by talking to other homeowners, meeting with your local finance company home buyers consultants to get an overview of expenses involved, then make a calculated decision and determine the amount of money you can afford to spend on being a homeowner. When you implement this strategy, you will be like the mound building ants that construct the hill they live in. You too will be able to have a place to call home and afford the upkeep.

3. Third Cause - You have lost hope

You started out full of zeal and then you let the trials and tribulations you experience bring on laziness. You aren't attaining your goals so you lost hope. You don't believe that things will turn around, you have your hope misplaced, you are not hoping in God anymore. I don't know where your hope is, but you and the Lord knows. **Proverbs 13:12** says "Hope deferred makes the heart sick but when desires cometh, it is a tree of life." You may have started out the year excited, hopeful and full of life.

You made resolutions to lose weight, write a book, start investing in stocks, purchase property or a home, get a more reliable vehicle, start a savings plan, etc. but some things got thrown into the equation that you didn't expect. The way you can counteract this laziness is by doing what **Romans 12:12** says "be joyful in hope, patient in affliction, faithful in prayer." I want you to be like the social ant and get social as a strategy for this.

STRATEGY: For instance, you had a goal to build up a savings account – get together with your family and friends and come up with something that you will use to generate extra income to build up this account. You'd be surprised of the creativity that comes out of your family and friends when you solicit them and they feel like they are going to be a part of something that will be life changing for you.

I know you've seen this on Oprah and other television programs where the need was announced and people from everywhere came to the rescue to be a part of bringing about a change in the life of a perfect stranger. This strategy brings joy to you and the persons helping out.

STATEGIST CASE STUDY

About 10 years ago, one way that 3 of my friends and I saved money was by having each one of us save $20 a pay period. You too can implement this same concept with 3 other people you trust. You can use the money which equates to $520 in a year to jump start your savings account. Each time you get extra money you should place it in this savings account. You will be surprised how achieving this goal will get you back to being hopeful.

At that time when I saved the $520, I had a goal in mind of purchasing an $800 watch I had been watching all year. I noticed how low it would go on sale which was $600. Instead of getting the watch on credit and paying interest to the jewelry company, I was earning interest in my savings account. Even though it wasn't a whole lot, I was able to pay cash for that watch.

Thank the Lord for patience. You also will be patient in affliction because your goal is not so high that it isn't attainable and the most pain that could be afflicted is the fact that you just won't be able to have something that you would have otherwise purchased with that $20. If you think about it, you probably don't need it anyway.

Also, you will be faithful in prayer because you know that God answers prayer. As He reveal to you the wisdom and strategies necessary for you to put into action to attain your goal and you begin to see results, you will want to spend more time in prayer. When you implement this strategy, you then will be like the social ant.

Now, I have a question for you? Are you a sluggard or a strategist? If you had been a sluggard, I want you to take time right now to repent and ask the Lord for forgiveness and to renew a right spirit in you. Thank the Lord for sending you a word through this teaching to pull you out of laziness and catapult you into the mindset of a strategist like the ant.

I already gave an example of how to start saving money by saving $20 a pay period but that was an example. So if this is a goal you want to accomplish, write it down on your worksheet and then write down how you will accomplish this each quarter. You may have the same concept for each quarter or it may vary. The objective is to tap into your creativity and devise a plan that is doable and produces results. Here are some reasons to devise a strategy to start saving money.

Reason 1: **Unforeseen Life Situations** – Review your Cash Flow Statement to see how you can reduce your expenses to begin to save at least 8 months to 1 year the amount of money it would take to keep things current if you were to lose your job or got sick and couldn't work for a while.

Reason 2: **College** - Your children may want to go to college to learn a new trade. The 529 College Plan is a great savings plan to setup. This is how it works: you will save a predetermined amount of money each month in this account based on your child's age and the cost of college for the year that you start the savings plan. For example, if your child is 5 years old, and you start this plan in 2011, you will be saving money for 12 years in this account. The great thing about this plan is that the cost of college for your child is locked in at the price of college for 2011 not the cost of college in 2023 which is when he/she will start college.

Reason 3: **Start A Business** – Starting a business is a way to have another stream of income that can eventually replace your job.

Reason 4: **Purchase Investment Property** – Owning property definitely will produce residual income. The most economical way to purchase property is through tax deed sales. Once you save up enough money to go to a sale and purchase the property, you then will own it free and clear. Now you can hold the mortgage on the property. Like T.D. Jakes said on one of his teachings, "it really does matter who gets the interest." You now will collect interest on that 30 year mortgage instead of a banking institution.

Reason 5: **Stocks** – There is money to be gained in purchasing stocks. I recommend that you read up on this concept before you get involved since you can also lose money if you don't know what you are doing.

Reason 6: **Retirement** – It is my heart's desire that you enjoy your retirement. You should save money in a Roth IRA account since it won't be taxed once you start getting it at retirement age. The other retirement savings you should invest in is a 401k plan that has a company match since that is free money saved on behalf of your employer.

Reason 7: **Be A blessing – Deut 15:11** says "For the poor shall never cease out of the land; therefore I command thee saying, thou shalt open thine hand wide unto they brother, to thy poor and to thy needy in thy land." So in lieu of this, in order for you to be a cheerful giver to the poor, you need to have money saved for times when the poor, elderly and children have need. **Proverbs 19:17** says "He that hath pity upon the poor lendeth unto the Lord and that which he hath given will he pay him again." How many of you love being on God's payroll? I do. I'll stop here for now. You may have a few other reasons of your own as to why you should start a savings plan.

CONCLUSION: I pray that you see why **Proverbs 6:6** says to consider the ant. Don't you just love the ant? And when you read the next verse, you will get empowered and motivated to move from being a sluggard to a strategist for **Proverbs 6:7** says "which having no guide, overseer or ruler provideth her meat in the summer and gathered her food in the harvest."

Now if the ant can accomplish its goal of reaping a harvest without a guide, ruler or overseer, surely being children of the most high God, we can accomplish our goals considering the fact that we have the Holy Spirit, as our guide, ruler and overseer. The concept behind being a 90/10 Steward is giving because of the love that we have towards God and each other. If you don't plant seeds, you will not be able to produce a harvest. As you spend time with God in prayer, He will reveal to you your perpetual harvest savings plan strategy in order for you to be like the ant – the strategist.

ASSIGNMENT: You will populate the "**My Perpetual Harvest Savings Plan Strategy**" worksheet. On this worksheet you will have four columns – one for each season – summer, winter, spring and fall. You will have several rows with goals that you want to accomplish for each season. You are to write down the strategies that you will implement to accomplish these goals for each season.

MY PERPETUAL HARVEST SAVINGS PLAN STRATEGY

SUMMER
GOAL_____

STRATEGY:

_____
_____
_____
_____

WINTER
GOAL_____

STRATEGY:

_____
_____
_____
_____

SPRING
GOAL_____

STRATEGY:

_____
_____
_____
_____

FALL
GOAL_____

STRATEGY:

_____
_____
_____
_____

10 HAVE YOU IMPLEMENTED PRUDENCE TO AVOID PUNISHMENT?

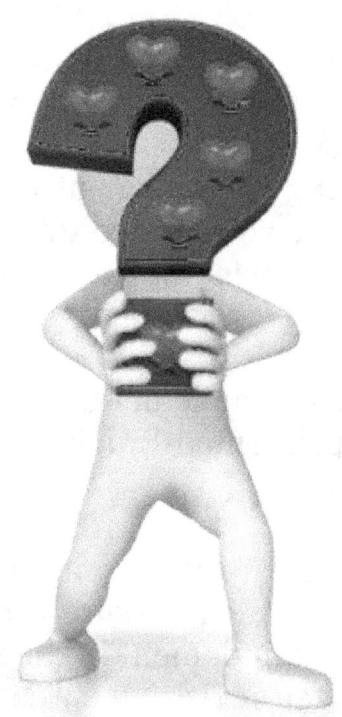

SCRIPTURE: **Proverbs 27:12** *"A prudent man sees evil and hideth himself; but the simple pass on and are punished."*

TOPIC: Our topic for today is Have You Implemented Prudence To Avoid Punishment?

PRAYER: Before we get started let's pray, dear Heavenly Father, thank you for this day, thank you for your word thank you for your continued grace and mercy. Give us the wisdom, knowledge and understanding necessary to implement prudence in our daily affairs. Let us continue to bring glory and honor to your name as 90/10 stewards, in Jesus name we pray, Amen.

REVIEW: In the previous chapter, we discussed the topic "let's consider the ant a strategist." In that teaching we looked at the 90/10 steward as a strategist. As an assignment, you were to create a worksheet "**My Perpetual Harvest Savings Plan Strategy**" to outline a savings plan. I also gave 7 reasons why you should start a savings plan.

On this worksheet you were to populate each of the four columns – one for each season – summer, winter, spring and fall with your savings goals that you want to accomplish for each season. You were to write down the strategies that you were going to implement to accomplish these goals for each season. For those of you who created this worksheet, you should have a testimony of how you have opened up an account so that you can begin working towards building it up for whatever goal you want to achieve.

In this chapter, we will discuss implementing prudence based on our topic for today of "Have You Implemented Prudence To Avoid Punishment? So let's get started.

PRUDENCE: First let's look at the definition of **prudence** according to Merriam Webster dictionary which is "shrewdness in the management of practical affairs, skill and good judgment in the use of resource and caution or circumspection as to danger or risk." As we go through this teaching, we will look at some of the practical financial affairs we should implement prudence with as 90/10 stewards to avoid danger, risk or punishment.

As we look at our scripture for today, we see that a prudent person sees evil and hides himself from it or does what is necessary to avoid it. Also from this same scripture we see that the simple person who sees evil and does nothing about it ends up suffering.

SIMPLE: The definition of **simple** according to Merriam Webster is "stupid, naïve, lacking in knowledge or expertise, not culturally sophisticated." Regardless to whether the simple are doing nothing because they just don't know what to do or just being plain old stupid and refuse to do the right thing, will give them the same end result which is punishment.

PUNISHMENT: The definition of **punishment** according to Merriam Webster Dictionary is suffering, pain or loss that serves as retribution; secondly it is severe, rough or disastrous treatment and thirdly it is penalty inflicted on an offender through judicial procedures.

With these thoughts in mind, I want to help you to operate as a prudent person instead of a simple minded person so that we can bring glory to God as we represent him here on earth as end time financiers and 90/10 stewards.

Now one of the reasons I gave to save money in the previous chapter was to **save money for unforeseen life situations**. In lieu of that, I want to talk to you about different insurances that you should have. Since we are children of the most high God, we have been empowered by the Holy Spirit with the wisdom necessary to implement prudence.

God's word is full of wisdom and He wants us to be responsible and implement wisdom in our daily financial affairs. Considering that the world is still experiencing economic turmoil, some may decide that they don't need insurance and others may have even lost their insurance policies because of job loss. But hopefully you can do as we talked about last month, start saving 9 to 12 months of money to cover your expenses so that you can have backup income for unforeseen situations such as illness, fire, theft, disability, death, car accidents and unemployment. As 90/10 stewards we are to take the time out to evaluate, research and plan out our insurance needs.

Here are some questions to ask to determine what your insurance needs are:
1. If you own a home, do you have insurance to cover any unforeseen damage if something tragic were to happen. Or, do you have renter's insurance if you are renting to protect again theft?
2. If you are married, do you have insurance for an unforeseen untimely

death of your spouse or even your children living with you?
3. If you encountered some kind of unforeseen health issue that disabled you, do you have insurance to cover the medical bills?
4. If you had a car accident, do you have insurance to cover the damage?

Some of these situations are ones that most people really don't like talking about and it is understandable but **Proverbs 23:4** says "yea though I walk through the valley of the shadow of death, I will fear no evil for though art with me thy rod and thy staff comfort me." And **2 Timothy 1:7** says "For God has not given us the spirit of fear but of power and of love and of a sound mind."

We are not to operate in fear and we don't want to let the enemy put it in our minds that if we have insurance that we aren't putting our trust and faith in God to protect us and provide for us. For we know that **Philippians 4:19** says "But my God shall supply all your need according to his riches in glory by Christ Jesus." So make sure to not put your trust in your insurance policies but in your provider which is Jesus Christ. Also, you should not put your hope and trust in your insurance vehicles for financial increase.

EXAMPLE:
If you have a million dollar policy on your spouse, you can't decide that you won't do anything else to secure your financial freedom in hopes of cashing in on that policy. I believe that God would rather bless you in so many other ways than because of some kind of tragedy or loss. The main thing to keep in mind about insurance is we are responsible to be good stewards over everything God has placed in our possession, which is our spouse, children, and assets.

So now that we know that we may encounter some kind of risk, let's talk about implementing wisdom to avoid the pain of not being prudent. I'm not saying that you won't experience pain if something happens to your possessions but I don't want you to add to the pain by not being financially prepared to deal with the loss.

There are three types of risk I want us to look at.

Risk One – Personal Risk

Personal risk involves the loss of our earning power through premature death or old age. **Hebrews 9:27** says "And as it is appointed unto men once to die, but after this the judgment." In order to address this risk, we need to implement prudence in the case of premature death or old age, by investing in a life insurance policy.

The purpose of getting life insurance is to provide for expenses which exist and to ensure that those left behind won't be burdened with those expenses. Existing expenses may include the cost of funeral arrangements, medical or hospital bills, mortgage balance on property owned, outstanding debt, children's education and welfare, and the ability to leave an inheritance to your children's children.

In order to determine the amount of insurance you will need, it is important to evaluate, the surviving spouse salary, income from the decedent's employee benefits, social security benefits, retirement and veteran's benefits.

Now this subject is near and dear to me since I lost my mom in 2009 and I thank the Lord that my mom was prudent because she had several life insurance policies in effect when she passed. We were able to have two funeral arrangements for her since she was living in Florida when she passed but wanted to be buried in New Orleans which is where she spent most of her life. She even carried life insurance on my three younger brothers since she worked for an insurance company and took advantage of the low rates.

Now that she has passed, my husband and I have taken over the policies that she had on my brothers. Of course you want to do your research on which company you would like to insure your family with so make sure to do your due diligence and check around on rates and terms based on your financial situation.

The other thing I want to talk about pertaining to this risk is that Christians should be better stewards when it comes to death **for Luke 16:18** says "and the Lord commended the unjust steward because he had done wisely for the children of this world are in their generation wiser than the children of light." Now this should not be so. At a minimum, you should at least get enough insurance to cover your burial expense. It definitely isn't a good testimony of a child of God if there is an unexpected death or even death of old age and the family have to scramble to get money together to bury their loved ones.

You don't want to just do the spiritual things, pray, worship, give, fellowship, witness, sing, usher and then have a raggedy testimony when it comes to natural things such as implementing prudence in your financial affairs. Keep in mind that 100% of what you are steward over belongs to God. The last thing on this subject is that you need to make sure the beneficiary information is up to date so that the payout of your policies won't be delayed.

EXAMPLE: One of my brothers passed before my mom but she had a policy with all 5 of her children listed as beneficiaries. Since she implemented prudence and removed him from the policy before she passed, the payout was divided by 4 of us instead of 5 when paid out on her death. For those of us who have older parents that aren't able to attend to their financial matters anymore, make sure that their policies are up to date so that they can have the proper burial they want to have.

Risk Two – Property Risk

Property risk involves the risk surrounding home ownership. For the most part, the most expensive item you will purchase will be your home. There are several ways we can implement prudence with home ownership. As good stewards of our blessings, we can protect our home by purchasing home owner's insurance to protect against things such as theft, loss, fire and income.

One way to protect our home is by investing in a security system. Not only will this help to ward off criminals but purchasing a security system will also help to lower your monthly payment for your homeowner's insurance policy. If you are going to purchase a security system, please utilize it. I know of a neighbor whose house was broken into even though there was an alarm system in place and they didn't bother to set the alarm.

So you can't just have an alarm system in your house only but you have to set it and get it connected with your local police and fire department system just in case you have a situation. Of course there is a monthly charge for this and some people may determine that they would rather just set the alarm to ward off thieves without having the police and fire department system notified. If this is the case, review your Monthly Cash Flow Statement to see where you can make adjustments so that you can incorporate this expense in your monthly cash flow statement.

The other thing you need to do is **get a video camera** and tape everything of value in your house and keep it in a safe place. It may be a good idea to have a backup copy that is kept maybe with another family member. The reason you want to do this is in case of a break in. You need to keep receipt of your items that are expensive and difficult to replace. Make sure to inform the insurance company of all of your high ticket priced jewelry, furs, art collections, etc.

The third protection that you can take advantage of for your home is getting the **insurance that will pay off your home** in case of a death or illness. This type of insurance is offered to you when you setup financing for the payment of your home. Now the thing I would like to mention about this type of protection on a personal level is that before my mom passed, my stepdad past five years earlier. They had 4 checks coming into the house before he passed but after he past, my mom only had her one check to live off of. Because of that, she wasn't able to continue living in the house they had since she couldn't afford the mortgage based on her one check.

Even though she had decent money left over from the policies she had on my stepdad, she did not use wisdom with it. She spent the money so fast and really didn't have anything to show for it in the end when we asked her what she did with all that money. She ended up losing her house and moving into a senior citizen community which was brand new and very nice but if she had a choice, she would have preferred to stay in her home.

So let's keep this in mind when we are choosing insurance. My mom could have done one of two things pertaining to securing her home after the death of a loved one. She could have opted to pay the extra money to carry the insurance that would have paid off the house in case of a death or she could have got some financial advice on how to use the money she received from the insurance policies to be able to keep her house. But for whatever reason, they chose not to purchase the insurance and she didn't implement financial principles with the money she received from the insurance policies.

Risk Three – Automobile Risk

Automobile risk involves the risk surrounding the purchase of a vehicle. This probably is the second most expensive item you will purchase. Risk involved with ownership of a vehicle involve unintentional injury of other person and/or yourself in case of an accident, damage to the other person's vehicle, bodily injury and lastly noncompliance with the law by driving a vehicle without proper coverage.

Having a nice vehicle is great and wonderful but first make sure you do your due diligence and find out how much it is going to cost monthly to carry automobile insurance on the vehicle before you purchase the vehicle. There are several companies you can purchase automobile insurance from so you will have to do research and find the most economical one to meet your needs in case you do have a situation.

There are so many Christians purchasing vehicles because they want to have the top of the line vehicles to appear blessed and highly favored. There's nothing wrong with that as long as you are able to make the payments and keep proper insurance on your vehicle. Now the law requires all vehicles to have insurance. So if you let your insurance lapse, there could be major suffering and pain because of it.

Once you let your insurance lapse, the insurance company notifies the department of motor vehicle. You then may end up getting your license suspended if you do not hurry up and get coverage. Once your license is suspended and you still choose to drive with no insurance and a suspended license and get stopped by the police for any reason, you will end up going to jail. This then will go on your record and you still will have to get insurance and pay the money to restore your license. This definitely is not a pretty picture or something you want to experience.

Risk Four – Health Risk

Health risk involves the risk with getting sickness, disease or disabled. Most jobs offer some type of health insurance. To implement prudence with this type of risk, you should definitely signup for health insurance when it is open season on your job unless you choose to get your insurance privately or through your spouse employer. Yes the premiums are high and yes co-pays are high and yes prescriptions are high.

Now to implement prudence with this type of risk, we are to keep in mind that our bodies are the temple of God according to **1 Corinthians 3:16** and we are to take care of our temple by eating right, getting proper rest and exercising. Our bodies were made to move.

I'm not saying that you need to go join a gym which would be good if you can but there are simple exercises you can do for 30 – 60 minutes a day such as jumping jacks, jumping rope, walking, running, lifting small hand weights, etc. This helps to keep your heart pumping and help to remove impurities out of your body naturally. Otherwise, if you don't eat a balance meal daily which includes eating 9 fruits and vegetables, get proper rest and exercise, you may end up with some kind of sickness, disease or disability.

Now I'm not saying if you do these things, you won't end up getting sickness, disease or disabled but these definitely are preventive measures that you can implement to try to remain healthy. Also a good practice if your body does get attacked, is to begin to **read scriptures on healing** and believe in the healing power of Jesus that is a part of your inheritance because of the finished work of Jesus Christ on Calvary.

Now that we have discussed these four risk factors, have you implemented prudence in these financial affairs? If you haven't, ask the Lord to give you the wisdom and the strength to do these things. Ask the Lord to forgive you of having the wrong mindset towards these things. Thank the Lord for this teaching and begin to implement a plan of action to start counteracting these risk.

CONCLUSION: I pray that you see how important it is to be a good steward over what God has placed in our possession by evaluating the risk involved with the things God has given you to steward. I pray that you have been empowered and motivated to implement prudence in your daily financial affairs now that you know what to do.

ASSIGNMENT: Your assignment is to populate the Insurance Management Worksheet titled "**My Insurance Policies Summary**". On this worksheet, you will populate the six columns with the Type of Insurance, the Premium Amount, the Term of the policy, the Annual Cost of the policy, the Renewal Premium Date and the name of the Insurance Agency holding the policy. You will have several rows for the type of insurance policies that you have purchased.

PRAYER: Dear Heavenly Father, thank you for your wisdom, knowledge and understanding. Thank you for your word, help us to implement prudence in our daily financial affairs. Help us as we meditate on your word daily so that it will empower us to implement kingdom strategies as you position us to be end time financiers for your kingdom here on earth as 90/10 stewards. I pray that you continue to send laborers to your vineyard so that we can reap the end time harvest of souls. In Jesus name Amen.

INSURANCE MANAGEMENT WORKSHEET

NAME: _____

INSURANCE POLICY SUMMARY
PROPERTY, AUTOMOBILE, HEALTH, LIFE

INSURANCE CO. _____
TYPE OF INSURANCE _____ FACE VALUE_____
PREMIUM AMT_____TERM_____ ANNUAL COST_____
BENEFICIARY_____

INSURANCE CO. _____
TYPE OF INSURANCE _____ FACE VALUE_____
PREMIUM AMT_____TERM_____ ANNUAL COST_____
BENEFICIARY_____

INSURANCE CO. _____
TYPE OF INSURANCE _____ FACE VALUE_____
PREMIUM AMT_____TERM_____ ANNUAL COST_____
BENEFICIARY_____

INSURANCE CO. _____
TYPE OF INSURANCE _____ FACE VALUE_____
PREMIUM AMT_____TERM_____ ANNUAL COST_____
BENEFICIARY_____

INSURANCE CO. _____
TYPE OF INSURANCE _____ FACE VALUE_____
PREMIUM AMT_____TERM_____ ANNUAL COST_____
BENEFICIARY_____

INSURANCE CO. _____
TYPE OF INSURANCE _____ FACE VALUE_____
PREMIUM AMT_____TERM_____ ANNUAL COST_____
BENEFICIARY_____

INSURANCE CO. _____
TYPE OF INSURANCE _____ FACE VALUE_____
PREMIUM AMT_____TERM_____ ANNUAL COST_____
BENEFICIARY_____

TOTAL LIFE INSURANCE: _____

11 ARE YOU OK WITH HAVING WEALTH & RICHES?

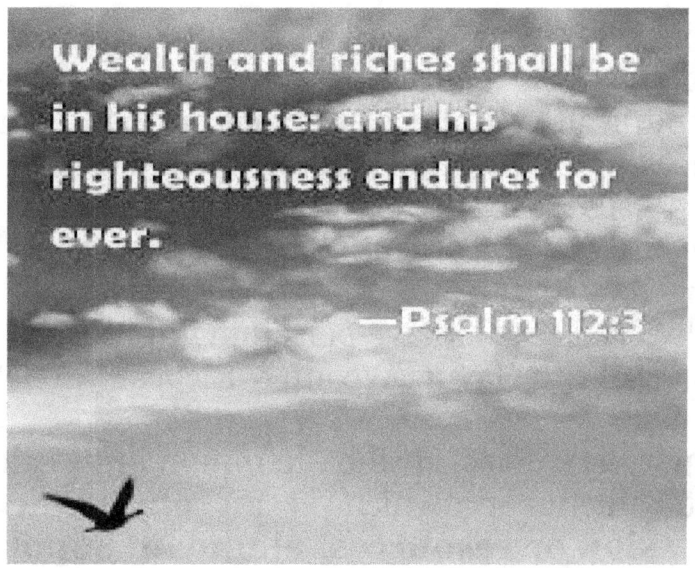

SCRIPTURE: **Psalms 112:1-3** *"Praise ye the Lord, blessed is the man that feared the Lord; that delighted greatly in his commandment. His seed shall be mighty upon the earth; the generation of the upright shall be blessed. Wealth and riches shall be in his house; and his righteousness endures forever."*

TOPIC: Are You Ok With Having Wealth & Riches?

PRAYER: Dear Heavenly Father, thank you for this day, thank you for your word thank you for your continued grace and mercy. Help us to get a better understanding of your promises of wealth and riches through your

Word so that we can possess those things that you have already predestined for us to have in order for us to continue to represent you as 90/10 stewards in your kingdom to bring glory to your name, in Jesus name we pray, Amen.

REVIEW: Now in the previous chapter, we continued by going over the concepts from "The 90/10 Steward, I Love Therefore I Give Workshop" and we talked on the subject "Have you implemented prudence to avoid punishment." In that teaching, we looked at the 90/10 steward as one who implements prudence in their financial affairs in the area of obtaining insurance.

As an assignment, you were to create an **"Insurance Management Worksheet"** to keep track of the various insurances you have for your home, car, life and health. I also elaborated on the importance of having these 4 insurances. For those of you who created this worksheet, you should have evaluated the various insurance and made adjustments accordingly to ensure that you are implementing prudence. Now let's delve into our training for this chapter. We will talk about wealth and the attitude or mindset you should have pertaining to it based on our topic for today of "Are You Ok With Having Wealth & Riches?" So let's get started.

WEALTH: First let's look at the definition of wealth according to Merriam Webster dictionary which is **an abundance of valuable material possession or resources, abundant supply, all property that has a money value or an exchangeable value**.

RICHES: According to Merriam Webster dictionary, the definition of riches is **things that make one rich – such as wealth.**

As we look at our scripture for today, we see that the person who fears the Lord is blessed. To fear the Lord is to have the right attitude, respect, honor and reverence towards God and his creation.

The reason the person who fears the Lord is blessed is because:
Proverbs 1:7 says the fear of the Lord is the beginning of knowledge - it is truly a blessing to have the Knowledge needed to know how to handle the wealth.

Proverbs 9:10 says the fear of the Lord is the beginning of wisdom - it is truly a blessing to have the wisdom needed to know how to obtain the wealth

Proverbs 10:27 says the fear of the Lord prolong days - it definitely is a blessing to be able to enjoy the wealth you have been blessed with

Proverbs 14:26 says in the fear of the Lord is strong confidence - it is definitely comforting knowing that your confidence is strengthened when you know for sure that you are operating in the gift that God has blessed you with to obtain wealth

Proverbs 14:27 says the fear of the Lord is a fountain of life - not only will you be blessed with an abundant life but you will also be able to bring life to others as you are a blessing to them

Proverbs 22:4 says by humility and the fear of the Lord are riches and honor and life - it is truly a blessing and humbling experience to know that the God who owns everything has chosen us to be stewards over the wealth that he has placed in our possession.

Eccl 12:13 says let us hear the conclusion of the whole matter, fear God and keep his commandments, for this is the whole duty of man.

LOVE IS THE FOUNDATION

So what are the commandments of God that we are to keep? Well I'm glad you asked so let's go to **Matthew 22:34-40** which reads "Hearing that Jesus had silenced the Sadducees, the Pharisees got together, One of them, an expert in the law, tested him with this question: "Teacher, which is the greatest commandment in the Law?" Jesus replied: "'Love the Lord your God with all your heart and with all your soul and with all your mind.' This is the first and greatest commandment . And the second is like it: 'Love your neighbor as yourself.' All the Law and the Prophets hang on these two commandments." Love is the foundation of everything; that is why this teaching is based on love.

So now that you love the Lord, the wealth and riches you have accumulated or will accumulate can be properly appropriated because of your love for Christ and his people. Before you had a relationship with Christ, you didn't have the strength, power or knowledge to give a dime out of a dollar or give to the poor or leave behind an inheritance to your children's children nor did you see God as your source therefore, you spent your money on what you wanted.

You may have even been selfish and stingy and could care less if anything was left behind once you were dead and gone. So let's thank the Lord right now for salvation and for loving us enough to give his life on Calvary for our sins and transgressions. And now that he has risen with all power in his hand, he has given us that same power to renew, revive and transform our mindset and attitude towards wealth and riches.

BIBLICAL WEALTH AND RICHES

Now let's review some of the wealth the people had in the Bible
Genesis 13:2 says And **Abraham** was very rich in cattle, silver and in gold.
Genesis 30:43 says and the man **(Jacob)** increased exceedingly and had much cattle, and maidservants and menservants and camels and asses.
Genesis 36:6 says And **Esau** took his wives, and his sons, and his daughters, and all the persons of his house, and his cattle, and all his beasts, and all his substance, which he had got in the land of Canaan; and went into the country from the face of his brother Jacob. For their riches were more than that they might dwell together; and the land wherein they were strangers could not bear them because of their cattle.
I Kings 4 and **Ecclesiastes 2** gives us a list of some of the wealth **Solomon** had such as houses, vineyards, pools, silver, gold, peculiar treasures, men singers, women singers, musical instruments, 40k stalls of hours, 12k horsemen, fig trees, barley and the list goes on and on.
Acts 16:14 says "And a certain woman named **Lydia**, a seller of purple – purple was a valuable color and chiefly worn by the princes and the rich.
Acts 4:34-35 says Neither was there any among them that lacked, for as many as were possessors of land and houses, sold them.

These are just a few examples of the blessings of the Lord given to his people and since you are Christ servants, you have access to the same blessings for **Galatians 3:29** says and if ye be Christ's , then are ye Abraham seed and heirs according to the promise.

As you read these scriptures in depth, you will see that it was the Lord who blessed these men with their wealth and riches for **Deuteronomy 8:18** says but thou shalt remember the Lord your God for it is he that giveth thee power to get wealth. Because of this, those who have accumulated wealth have gotten to implement wisdom in order to be a good steward over it. To sum it all up we'll read **Proverbs 10:22** which says the blessings of the Lord, it maketh rich and added no sorrow. So it is ok for us to have wealth and riches.

TWENTY FIRST CENTURY WEALTH AND RICHES

Now that we are ok with having wealth and riches, let's look at some of the wealth and riches that we have in the 21st century to be stewards over. I'm going to go over some of the riches that wealthy people may have in their portfolio. Some of these you may have now or none at all but I'm going to decree and declare that you will in the near future.

These are assets that you should have in the 21st century:

1) CASH
2) BONDS
3) MONEY MARKET ACCOUNT
4) MUTUAL FUNDS
5) REAL ESTATE
6) NAUTRAL RESOURCES SUCH AS OIL & GAS

7) GOLD
8) SILVER
9) STOCKS
10) A BUSINESS
11) TREASURY BILLS
12) CD

Your financial portfolio should be a diversified portfolio meaning that you should have several streams of income to help control risk. Now I am not a certified financial planner but my husband and I are certified financial literacy educators. So when deciding on how to diversify your wealth, it is best to consult a professional preferably one who fears the Lord. What I want to do is expose you to the different investment platforms available for you to consider as investment vehicles.

So let's talk about these different investment vehicles.

Cash - We have already discussed in one of our previous teachings that you should have a savings account with 8-12 months of emergency funds. This account should be a high yield interest rate account. You can go to bankrate.com and find the best financial institution to meet this requirement.

Bonds – A bond is a debt security similar to an I.O.U. So when you purchase a bond, you are lending money to a government, corporation, federal agency or other entity known as an issuer. In return for that money, the issuer provides you with a bond in which it promises to pay a specified rate of interest during the life of the bond and to repay the face value of the bond when it matures. An example is when I worked for the government, I would buy $50 bonds every pay period at a cost of $25. Now in order for me to get the face value of $50, I had to hold that bond at least 8 to 10 years. Bonds are considered stable, safe and dependable.

Stocks – Stocks represent ownership in a company. When you own stock in a company, you are called a shareholder and entitled to your share of the company's earnings as well as any voting rights attached to the stock. When you own shares of stock in a company, you will receive a stock certificate which is a piece of paper showing proof of ownership and the number of shares you own. Since there is a much higher risk in purchasing stocks, you need to do research, research and research before you invest in a company. By being a stock owner you are assuming the risk of the company not being successful. So if the company files bankrupt or liquidate, you may not get any money but on the brighter side if the company does well, you can earn a lot of money.

Mutual Funds – It is a collection of stocks and/or bonds and other securities invested by a group of people. Each investor owns shares which represent a portion of the holdings of the funds. There are 3 ways you can make money from mutual funds: 1) is income earned from dividends on stocks and interest on bonds 2) capital gains if the funds sell and 3) When the Fund holdings increase.

Real Estate – We talked about this in one of the previous teachings but there are several ways to have residual income with real estate. You can purchase tax deed certificates, tax deeds, a single family home, an apartment complex, a strip mall, vacant land, farm land or even commercial property. The way you earn money with tax deed certificates is by earning interest. With tax deeds, you can out right own the the property free and clear and with other real estate you can earn money by collecting rent or lease the property. And if you own the property you can hold the mortgage and have your purchaser get financing from you so you are paid the monthly mortgage instead of a bank.

Business – We talked about tapping into our creativity in one of our previous teaching and how you can start a business. You can start a business part-time initially to produce extra income or if you are unemployed, you can run your business full-time. The beauty about starting a business is that you can pass it down throughout several generations.

Once you have wealth through these various concepts, you need to have the wisdom and knowledge necessary to know how to be a good steward with it – and the way you are to obtain this wisdom and knowledge is by having the fear of the Lord as indicated by the scriptures we just read. You are going to need to know how to multiply your wealth through investing it properly. You are going to need to have discernment with it so that you can sow it into good soil where it will reproduce. Applying good stewardship positions your wealth to be passed down to your children's children.

Did you hear me mention, a car, clothes, the latest gadget, some type of medication for high blood pressure or diabetes as a form of wealth generation? No! You didn't because none of these are investment vehicles unless you are investing in the makers of these products such as Mercedes, Nike, Apple or Cardinal Health. So make sure that you will receive a return on your investment instead of investing in depreciating assets such as clothes, cars, etc.

You don't want to be called a wicked servant like the person in the parable of the talents in **Matthew 25:14-46**. I'm not going to read it for the sake of time but here's a summation of it: Jesus illustrated two different types of stewards - those who were a good steward because they multiplied what they were steward over and a wicked steward because he operated in fear and did nothing with the talent he was given. We are not to operate in fear but in faith. Now because this wicked steward operated in fear and did not invest the talent he was steward over, it was taken from him. We don't want this to happen to us as 90/10 stewards.

CONCLUSION: If you wondered why I titled this teaching "are you ok with having wealth and riches", I want you to know that as 90/10 stewards and end time financiers:

- ❖ you will have wealth and riches in your house,
- ❖ you will be the head and not the tail,
- ❖ you will be a lender and not a borrower,
- ❖ you will own houses, lands and vineyards,
- ❖ you will lend to the poor,
- ❖ you will cloth the naked,
- ❖ you will feed the hungry,
- ❖ you will be a cheerful giver,
- ❖ everything you put your hands to do will prosper,
- ❖ you will fear the Lord in order to have a continuous flow of grace and mercy following you all the days of your life as you heed to the commands of the Lord
- ❖ and you will love the Lord your God with all your heart, mind, soul and strength and love your neighbor accordingly.

WHY DO WE NEED WEALTH? We need wealth because:

- it takes money to keep the church doors open,
- it takes money to get the Word preached and taught on tv and radio,
- it takes money to have a Christian academy,
- it takes money to assist those in need of food, shelter, clothing, education and jobs.

This is not about you, this is about establishing God's kingdom here on earth according to the Lord's prayer which says "thy kingdom come, thy will be done on earth as it is in heaven." Now do you believe what you pray or is it just done out of ritual, habit or religion?

Are you tired of seeing saints struggling, just barely making it and looking like they don't belong to the King of Kings and the Lord of Lords, the one who owns the cattle on a thousand hills, the earth and the fullness thereof?

It is time for the wealth to be transferred and I believe that time is now. The Lord has brought this teaching to you for such a time as this – it is harvest time – it is time to reap the end time harvest of souls before Jesus returns.

You may be thinking who does she think I am? Chelsea Clinton or the Hilton girls? No, I know who you are but do you? You are a royal priesthood, a holy nation, you are the child of the most high God, there is nothing too hard for your Heavenly Father. Let your petition be known to the Lord because He not only hears your prayers but He also answers prayers. I don't want my children to say "where be all the miracles our forefathers told us about."

Our children are going to see miracles, signs and wonders. As you take heed to these teaching as a 90/10 steward and create your different worksheets given in each of these chapters, you and your family will be able to look back and see how the Lord brought you through in the midst of a famine. This testimony can be passed down from generation to generation. My mom left a financial testimony for me to pass down to my kids and they definitely will have my testimony to pass down to my grandchildren.

This is a new season and a new day. It is time to reap the harvest of souls through the love that we are going to demonstrate in word as well as deed. When this type of love is received, the lost can't help but want to know where this love comes from. This will definitely open the door for you to tell the good news of Jesus to them. It is time out for playing church – we have to be the church.

So whatever you need to do to transition over to having the mind of Christ, do it. If you have to repent, do it, if you have to study God's word more, do it, if you have to increase your prayer time, do it, if you have to fast, do it, if you need to re-evaluate your cash flow statement and see where you can make adjustments do it – bottom line: it is time for us to possess the wealth and riches that the Lord wants us to have. So I'm telling you the same thing Jesus mother told the servants in **John 2:5** when they ran out of wine at the wedding in John 2:5 which reads "His mother said to the servants, do whatever He tells you."

ASSIGNMENT: Your assignment for this lesson will be to create a **Wealth Wheel Worksheet**. You will populate this wealth wheel with the investment vehicles we discussed that you have invested in with the following examples: Investment Vehicle Ex: AIG Stock, Investment Company Ex:ShareBuilder, Investment Amount: Ex: $1000, Investment Term Ex: 6 months, Investment Gain /Loss Ex: +100/-100. You will do this for each investment - bonds, stocks, mutual funds, real estate and business.

PRAYER: Dear Heavenly Father, thank you for your wisdom, knowledge and understanding. Thank you for blessing us to be a blessing. Thank you for being a God of promise. As we enter in prayer, give us revelation of how to obtain the wealth and riches that you already predestined for us to have. Help us to be good stewards over everything you bless our hands to do as end time financiers so that we can reap the end time harvest of souls. I pray that if anyone participating in this teaching does not know the Lord Jesus Christ as Saviour, I pray that you will accept him as Lord & Saviour because of his finished work on the cross of dying for your sins so that you can live your life for Him. In Jesus name Amen.

WEALTH WHEEL WORKSHEET

YEAR:_____NAME: _____

INVESTMENT VEHICLE Ex: Stocks	INVESTMENT COMPANY Ex: ShareBuilder	INVESTMENT AMOUNT Ex: $1000	INVESTMENT TERM Ex: 6 months	INVESTMENT GAIN/LOSS Ex: +100/-100
1.				
2.				
3.				
4.				
5.				
6.				
7.				
8.				
9.				
10.				

TOTAL: _____ _____ _____

Terri B. Jones

12 YES YOU HAVE SOMETHING TO SOW, BUT WILL IT BE SPARINGLY OR BOUNTIFULLY

SCRIPTURE: **II Corinthians 9:6-9** *"But this I say, He which soweth sparingly shall reap also sparingly; and he which soweth bountifully shall reap also bountifully. Every man according as he purposeth in his heart, so let him give; not grudgingly, or of necessity: for God loveth a cheerful giver. And God is able to make all grace abound toward you; that ye, always having all sufficiency in all things, may abound to every good work: (As it is written, He hath dispersed abroad; he hath given to the poor: his righteousness remaineth for ever)."*

TOPIC: Yes You Have Something to Sow, but Will it be Sparingly or Bountifully?

PRAYER: Dear Heavenly Father, thank you for this day, thank you for your Word and thank you for being our provider. Help us to see that we do have something to sow so that we can be fruitful, multiply, subdue, replenish and dominate in every arena that you strategically place us in. Now let us bring glory and honor to your name as 90/10 stewards as we establish your kingdom here on earth, in Jesus name we pray, Amen.

REVIEW: In the previous chapter, we discussed the topic "**Are You Ok With Having Wealth & Riches.**"   In that teaching, we looked at the 90/10 steward attitude and mindset pertaining to wealth.   As an assignment, you were to create a "**Wealth Wheel Worksheet**". On this wealth wheel you were to write down the different investment vehicles you want to invest in such as cash, bonds, stocks, mutual funds, real estate and business. For those of you who created this worksheet, you should have an overview of your goals you want to attain pertaining to wealth.   Now let's move on to this chapter's training.

TIME, TALENT, TREASURE: We will talk about sowing seed of our time, talent and treasure based on our topic "Yes You Have Something To Sow, but Will it be Sparingly or Bountifully? So let's get started.

SPARINGLY: First let's look at the definition of sparingly according to Merriam Webster dictionary which is "**marked by or practicing careful restraint as in the use of resources and careful use of one's money.**"

BOUNTIFULLY: The definition of bountifully according to Merriam Webster dictionary is "**liberal in bestowing of gifts or favors and given or provided abundantly a bountiful harvest.**"

TIME • TALENT • TREASURE

The three most important and valuable assets I believe we have been blessed with and given as seed to sow is our time, talent and treasure. Let's take a look at these three assets in relations to sowing of them sparingly or bountifully.

Time

Now as far as time is concerned, your **time** is very valuable and you can choose to sow of your time sparingly or bountifully – I know you've heard the saying before or you may have even said it yourself that "time is money". Example: Your salary is based on the time you put in at your job. So if you normally work 8 hours, you get 8 hours of pay. Then there are times when your job may need workers to volunteer to work extra hours.

When you work the extra hours, you can get paid time and a half or even double time. So in relationship to sowing of this time sparingly or bountifully, you can see that you can reap more income by sowing of your time past your normal work hours which will result in a bountiful harvest on your upcoming paycheck. Or you can decide to sow of your time sparingly with this situation because you have determined that the extra money isn't worth your time. Remember that the definition of sparingly is the **careful restraint of the use of your resources**.

Talent

Let's look at the second valuable asset, our **talent** – Your talent is the thing that you are naturally wired up to do, you're really good at it and others see it in you also. Normally it is derived from the use of your five senses, your hand, eyes, ears, nose or throat. It is sad to say that some people don't know what their talent is. Even worse than that is the one who knows what their talent is but isn't reaping a bountiful harvest. Normally when someone tells me that they know of someone who is looking for a job and ask if I know if anybody is hiring, the first thing I ask is what are they good at doing – which is the same as saying what is that person's talent.

Example: I have a neighbor who's grandson was visiting and he was telling me that he didn't see the value of going to college since he can get paid just as much money fixing on cars without a degree. So I asked him if he was fixing on cars and he said he was doing it on the side because nobody is hiring.

So even though he knows he is really good at this, he isn't reaping a bountiful harvest since he doesn't understand that he can get a specialized degree as a mechanic and instead of just making money on the side or sparingly, once he has his certification he will be able to get hired as a mechanic and paid accordingly. He then will be able to reap a bountiful harvest since he can still fix cars on the side and at a mechanic shop as well.

Treasure

Our third valuable and important asset is our treasure. Our **treasure** consist of the things that we possess of monetary value such as cash, gold, silver, houses, land, stocks, bonds, etc. The reason I used treasure is because most people can relate to the fact that treasure can be stored up or hoarded. When it is hoarded, it definitely is used sparingly but the fact that you are able to store up money in a high interest yielding savings account, in stocks or bonds, etc. you definitely can reap bountifully from these concepts.

As we look at our scripture for today, we see that the person who gives sparingly will also reap sparingly. So if we know this, why do you think some people sow sparingly of their time, talent and treasure? Well, I don't know what your thoughts are so I'm going to give you just a few reasons why I believe people sow sparingly and then give you some ways that they can begin to sow of them bountifully:

SOWING OF YOUR TIME

When it comes to sowing of time sparingly, I believe that person doesn't know how to make good use of certain appointed times in their lives. God is in charge and He knows the thoughts he has towards you which are good and not evil. There are set times for things to happen in your life according to **Ecclesiastes 3:1** which says "There is a time for everything and a season for every activity under the sun." Before you can know how to sow of your time productively, you are going to have to spend time with God to get revelation of how He wants you to make good use of your time to be a blessing to yourself, your family and the kingdom of God. **Ecclesiastes 8:5** says "Whoso keepeth the commandment shall fear no evil thing and a wise man's heart discerned both time and judgment."

Here are some things you can do to sow of your time bountifully:

1.Spend Time Reading God's Word

Determine a set time of day to read God's Word in order to equip yourself with the Word to counteract the schemes of the devil. It will also equip you to do the work of ministry. You will begin to know who you are in Christ. Not only will this practice build up your spirit man but you also will be able to encourage others by reminding them of God's promises and blessings through His Word. The best thing that you will gain out of this is the wisdom and boldness to win others to Christ. **Proverbs 11:30** says "the fruit of the righteous is a tree of life and he that winneth souls is wise."

As I talk about this, I am reminded of a friend of mine who I used to walk to school with every morning. Her dad held Bible study with us every morning before we left for school. It was very refreshing and uplifting for me since my dad was an alcoholic and didn't have a relationship with Christ.

2.   Spend Time With Your Family

In order to bond with your family and create family memories to look back on, spend quality time with your family listening to their thoughts and expression of the things they experienced throughout the day.   This is a valuable and priceless use of your time. As you do this, you will put a smile on their face as you share your wisdom to put a positive light on the negative situations they encounter. Once your kids are gone and grown, they will be able to reflect on these times with their families even after you are long gone.

EXAMPLE: A few years ago I called my cousin who turned 50 on Halloween. She began to tell me that she is a diabetic now and how she has to eat more vegetables. She said that as she was talking to her mom about how she has to eat more vegetables, they begin to laugh as they reminisced about how I used to eat everybody's vegetables at the table when none of the adults were looking. So take advantage of this precious time you have with your family. **Proverbs 17:22** says "A merry heart doeth good like a medicine but a broken spirit dries the bones."

3.   Spend Time At Your Local Church

You can be an asset in the furtherance of the gospel as you donate your time to the things that are needed at your local church. You can attend prayer meetings and be a blessing to others in need of someone to be a prayer partner. When your church has special services, you can help by being hostess to some of the people coming in from other towns. You can help by being present during regular times of fellowship. This is important since people are able to watch church services on tv and over the internet. **Psalms 111:1** says "Praise ye the Lord. I will praise the Lord with my whole heart in the assembly of the upright and in the congregation."

So when it comes to sowing of your time, keep in mind that as you sow sparingly of your time, you will reap sparingly. Who knows when the day will come when you may need someone to spend time with you in prayer as you go through your test, trials and tribulations? You may need someone to talk to about your failures and successes to encourage you along the way. And then who knows when you are going to want support of your church family as you operate in the gift that God has blessed you to do in ministry. With this in mind, let us do the things that will have us to reap bountifully as we sow our time.

Sowing of Your Talent

I believe that the reason some people sow their talent sparingly is because many people have lost their jobs or businesses during this economic down turn. Because of this they have lost their motivation and don't feel a sense of value or worth – I am here to remind you that you have been blessed with that talent for a reason – **Proverbs 16:18** says "A man's gift maketh room for him and bringeth him before great men." So use this time to hear from God to see how you can use your talent to be a blessing to his kingdom as He prepares you to go before great men.

Here are some things that you can do to sow of your talent **bountifully**:

1. Discover Your Talent As You Read God's Word

The Bible is full of examples of people who were talented. Also you can read books written by men and women of God that will help you to discover what your talent is – I read a book a few years ago called *Discover Your Purpose In 10 Days by Catherine Eagan.* What that book showed me is that I am gifted to teach. This is something that I have been doing since I was 13 years old. I not only teach in the natural or secular world but also in my local church.

So, just as you have been blessed to use your talent in the secular world, have you thought about ways that you can use that same gift in the body of Christ? **I Corinthians 12:28** says "And God has set some in the church first apostles, secondarily prophets, thirdly teachers after that miracles, then gifts of healing, helps, government, diversity of tongues." As you spend time in the Word, the Lord will give you revelation of how you can use that same talent he has blessed you with in the natural within the body of Christ.

2. Share Your Talent With Your Family

If you are a mechanic, cook, artist, computer programmer, financial officer, show your children, nieces and nephews how to do what the Lord has blessed you to do. You can even sign up with the local community college to teach your specialized skill for a small fee. You can book a room at your local library to introduce people in your community to your craft or trade so that when they need someone to do a job, you are the person they think about as the "go to" person. You do not have to be afraid that someone is going to take your talent and become better than you – keep in mind that we are to be fruitful, multiply, replenish, subdue and dominate according to **Genesis 1:28**. You will be able to bountifully reap from your talent as you train others how to do what you do and earn royalties or fees as you franchise your talent.

3. Utilize Your Talent In Your Local Church

All churches have the same need. The church need someone to keep the church looking good on the outside, to clean the church inside, do clerical work as a receptionist, play instruments, teach Sunday School classes. They need someone to hold workshops and seminars to teach the community about eating right, exercising and finances, video recording and all kind of technical skills needed for streaming the service online, interacting with people on social media sites about the church, and the list goes on and on.

So if you aren't employed, you can sow your talent to the local church. This will also help you stay on top of your game so that your skill will be fresh and you won't get rusty. Have you ever had somebody who used to bake the best sweet potato pie stop baking it for years and then you get to bragging about this pie to some people and ask her to make it and it doesn't taste like it used to? I'm going to suggest that this sister serve in the food ministry in the church in order to keep the recipe fresh in her mind and so that she can keep her title as the sweet potato pie queen.

If you are a beautician or a barber, offer to cut some little boy's hair or wash and set some of the kids hair for free, this will definitely be a blessing and a savings to the parent. Who knows, you may end up with some new customers as you sow of your talent.

Sowing of Your Treasure

I believe that a person sows sparingly of their treasure because that person has his eyes on his limited resources. I am here to let you know that there is no limit in our God. A great example is in **Matthew 14:17-18** which says "And they said unto him, we have here but 5 loaves and 2 fishes. He said bring them hither to me." This is what the Lord wants you to do. Give him your limited resources and watch him make it limitless. He wants you to look to him not look at what he has given you with your natural eyes.

If you have ever played any card game, you know that you can get a great hand to play sometimes and then there are times when you just want to throw in the hand because you see no way that you can win. Just as you have a partner to help you win in playing a card game, you have the Holy Ghost to help you to see your resources with renewed eyes.

Here are some things that you can do to sow of your treasure bountifully:

1. Read God's Word To Know When To Sow

To move into sowing bountifully of your treasure, you are going to have to know what the Word says pertaining to sowing and reaping, blessings and cursings and obedience and sacrifices. Once you get revelation of these commands and ordinances you will do what it says in **Ecclesiastes 11:6** which says "Sow your seed in the morning, and at evening let not your hands be idle, for you do not know which will succeed, whether this or that, or whether both will do equally well."

You cannot doubt, you cannot be in unbelief and you cannot operate in fear. None of these will produce the harvest that you really want instead know of a surety that God's Word is true, believe his promises and increase your faith as your spirit man grows knowing that God is in control.

2. Teach Your Family About Finances

As you encounter lean times, let this be a time to teach your family how to trust God instead of going out and get into debt. Sit down with the family and discuss ways that you all can make adjustments to weather this season in order to still have your needs met. This is when creative is at its finest. Play a game with your family. Let them know that you are going to give each person a weekend to plan what the family will eat and do for fun on a limited budget. You can give them the amount that you have determined is necessary.

Having the kids participate gives them a sense of ownership and makes this transition more adaptable for everyone. Who knows, your kids may come up with a dish that can used by other families such as 5 ingredient dinners or $25 a week food, family and fun kit. You may even decide to grow your own vegetables and sell them.   This definitely will position you to sow bountifully as you reap extra income.

3. Sow Your Treasure To Your Local Church

As 90/10 stewards, we are to give because of the love that Christ has for us. As we look at **II Corinthians 9:7** which says "Every man according as he purposeth in his heart, so let him give; not grudgingly, or of necessity." You should have purposed in your heart to give before you go to church. Your purpose should be centered on **Malachi 3:10** which says "Bring ye all the tithes and offering to the storehouse so that there may be meat in my house."

Now the Lord does not want his house to lack any thing that may be of need to his people. So in order to move to bountiful giving of your treasure, you have to see the needs of people through the eyes of Jesus. When you do this, you will take whatever you have and sow it and it will increase, it will multiply. Now some of you may not be employed; but you are getting income from somewhere. You may be getting unemployment, you may be getting food stamps, you may be getting a social security check. Yes you can sow of these things.

EXAMPLE: Just as the widow woman in **I Kings 17:10** gave to the man of God as the Lord commanded her, you can do the same thing. Because of her obedience, she reaped bountifully for **I Kings 17:15** says "And she went and did according to the sayings of Elijah and she, he and her house did eat many days." As you change your mind set about giving, you will see that as you take care of God's house, he will take care of yours. Here's an idea for those who receive food stamps, you can cook extra food and invite others over after fellowship as a way of sowing. That person you invited over may have asked the Lord during service to provide them a meal and guess what, he provided to them through you. Or as you take advantage of the buy one, get one free sales at the grocery store, be a blessing to a widow by creating a love basket with all of the free items.

CONCLUSION: There are 3 things that we have been given to sow of which is our time, talent and treasure. We are to read God's word to understand what God's Word has to say about sowing these things. Second, we are to sow these things into our family to leave an inheritance and then lastly we are to sow of these things in our local church to establish God's kingdom here on earth in order to reap the end time harvest of souls.

Monetary blessings definitely is a result of sowing and reaping but you also will reap of heavenly things for **II Corinthians 9:8-9** says "And God is able to make all grace abound toward you; that ye, always having all sufficiency in all things, may abound to every good work: (As it is written, He hath dispersed abroad; he hath given to the poor: his righteousness remaineth for ever.)" So let's tap into our God given creativity and look at ways that we can sow bountifully of our time, talent and treasure in order to continue giving to the poor and those in need.

ASSIGNMENT: You are going to populate the "**My Time, Talent and Treasure Worksheet**". On this worksheet you are going to write down ways that you can sow of your time, talent and treasure to reap a bountiful harvest as you read the Word of God, Interact With Your Family and friends and serve in your local church ministry.

PRAYER: Dear Heavenly Father, thank you for your wisdom, knowledge and understanding. Thank you for blessing us with the time you have given us here on earth. Thank you for revealing the talent that is already in us and help us to do the things that are necessary for the building up of your kingdom. Thank you for your promises. Help us to be good stewards of the heavenly treasure you bestow upon us daily as end time financiers so that we can reap the end time harvest of souls.

ABOUT US

Vision: Empower and enlighten the body of Christ to live out their financial potential and trust God as He supernaturally use us to fund the Kingdom of God for the end time harvest of souls and enforce His rule over all creation.

Philosophy: We must implement biblical and practical strategies through the love of God to one another in obedience to the Word of God as faithful and wise stewards over 100% of what we possess.

Mission: Teach the body of Christ through the Word of God, the 3 key strategies to empower them to lovingly give to God, themselves and others, become debt free and redirect those same resources to build generational wealth in order to reap the end time harvest of souls.

About Us: Ministers Thomas and Terri Jones have been brought into the kingdom for such a time as this to help the body of Christ lay the financial foundation necessary to make an impact on the kingdom of God, develop a unique plan of action and leave a legacy to our children's children as end time financiers.

Thomas and Terri are the owners of TJ & TJ Insurance Agency LLC, several investment properties, and founders of Create A Prayer Pillow, Track It! Slips, TJ&TJ Enterprise Internet Marketing Services, End Times Publishing LLC and The 90/10 Steward I Love Therefore I Give Financial Teaching Workshop.

Thomas H. Jones, a native of Bainbridge, Georgia has served eight years in the US Navy and 17 plus years in Management. Thomas has been a licensed minister since 1996 and has preached throughout Florida, Georgia and Alabama. Thomas held the first outdoor prison ministry in Greenville, Alabama. He has ministered on radio, television, at workshops, seminars, conferences and talk shows.

Terri B. Jones, affectionately known as "The Pillow Lady" is the mother of 4 young adults, wife of Minister Thomas H. Jones and "Grandma Chickee" to several grandchildren. Terri is a native of New Orleans, LA. She is a Motivational Speaker and Teacher, Entrepreneur and Author. She loves to cook, workout, play fun games and help others tap into their God given creativity. She has resided in Jacksonville, FL for over 30 years.

Terri accepted the Lord and has had a relationship with Christ for over 40 years. During these 40 years, Terri has faithfully operated in a range of gifts within the church as well as throughout the community.

She has been teaching 4, 5 and 6 year olds in youth ministries and an intercessor in intercessory prayer ministries for more than 20 years. Terri's creativity coupled with her gift to teach has taught educational and spiritual curriculums with engagement and enthusiasm in marketplace ministry, on the job, live radio, television, at workshops, seminars and conferences.

She has a Bachelors Degree in Business Information Systems and has been employed by Florida Blue formerly Blue Cross Blue Shield Of Florida for 30 years in Information Technology.

Terri is a reader at Daniel Kids and active member of nonprofit organization Womenade of Jacksonville, on the Board of Directors for nonprofit organization Pride In Action Community Services and a volunteer for Get Covered America.

She is the author of Let's Talk To The Hand, Drop & Give Him Sixty, End Times Daily Prayer Journal, Happy Father's Day Super Hero, Cat Salim Gets Her Wish, Turn Enjoyable Family Fun Crafts Into Cash, Here's How to Write a Book and Publish It, Bishop Is Preaching On Money Instructional Workbook, The 90/10 Steward - I Love Therefore I Give Financial Fun Teaching Workshop and3 Steps To Create MP3 Files Using Audacity EBook. Through End Times Publishing, she has published Plant the Word Each Day Children's Book for author Patricia Williams and The Weight Loss Diet That Is Free for author Deborah Ross.

www.ingramcontent.com/pod-product-compliance
Lightning Source LLC
Chambersburg PA
CBHW080809180526
45168CB00006B/2377

9 781517 743956